SELECTIONS FROM THE WRITINGS OF WILLIAM STEWART

(GAVROCHE)

Introductory Note

Few men of his time were more loved and respected than William Stewart—Willie, as he was affectionately known to a wide circle of comrades and friends. Born in Dunfermline (Fife) on 8th July, 1856, he was cradled in poverty and left fatherless as a mere child. Out of that poverty, pain, and suffering came the man that, by voice and pen, was to exercise an immense and wonderful influence on the common folk of Scotland and further afield.

A 2d. per week library in the linen mill in Dunfermline in which he worked as a youth took him into the land of literature, and soon he was a voluminous reader of the best in prose and poetry. In the early 80's of last century he crossed from radicalism to socialism—into the school of William Morris. For many years he was a contributor to the "Clarion" under Blatchford's editorship, and to the "Labour Leader" under Keir Hardie. Later, he was a regular contributor to "Forward" until within a few years of his death in Glasgow, on 27th August, 1947, aged 91.

For over 25 years Willie was secretary and organiser of the Independent Labour Party in Scotland, travelled all over the country breaking new ground, and laid the foundation of the socialist movement in Scotland. And all the time his pen was busy winning recruits, delighting thousands of readers of socialist magazines, at home and abroad, with his unique and masterly presentation of the case for socialism in the best literary style.

Here, then, in this little volume are three selections representative of his writings, to help hold the memory of a most lovable man—a man with never a thought of self or of the world's glittering prizes—a man of vision and understanding—a man of the common people and their loyal and devoted servant. JAMES W. TAYLOR

Glasgow.

August, 1948.

BOOK ONE

Robert Burns and the Common People

BIBLIOGRAPHICAL NOTE
First published (Reformers' Bookstall) 1910
New Edition, January, 1925

"My Compeers, the Common People."

—BURNS.

"He came when poets had forgot
How rich and strange the human lot;
How warm the tints of Life; how hot
Are Love and Hate;
And what makes Truth divine, and what
Makes Manhood great."

—WILLIAM WATSON.

"I am one of the sons of little men."

—BURNS.

ROBERT BURNS was born at Alloway, near Ayr, January 25, 1759.

The first edition of his poems was published at Kilmarnock in 1786.

The second edition was published at Edinburgh, 1787.

Editions innumerable have been published since all over the English-speaking world.

He died at Dumfries, July 21, 1796, just ten years from the publication of his first edition.

He was born in poverty, and he died in poverty. But he enriched the world.

FOREWORD

A foreword is never a foreword. It is an afterthought. It is the last thing written, and would be described as a postscript were it not that it is placed at the beginning instead of at the end. A foreword is an indication that the author, having written his book, has now begun to have doubts as to whether he has not been wasting his time. I have no such doubts. I think this is a good and necessary book, and does not stand in need of any postscriptive foreword. I have observed that the foreword to a book is usually either explanatory or apologetic. Sometimes it is both. Mine will be neither. The book will be its own explanation. And as for apology, I have none to offer. I shall most certainly continue to think that it is a good book, though all the readers and all the reviewers should think otherwise. Why should I apologise for having produced a good book?

This, then, is the Foreword:

I hope that what I have written will prove to be stimulative of thought concerning the relation of Burns' work to the present time; and even if the stimulus arises through resentment or antagonism to the ideas expressed, the writer's purpose will still have been achieved. If, on the contrary, my book be not stimulative, then I shall agree it had better not have been written.

WILLIAM STEWART.

CONTENTS

The Old Scots World

There has been much disputation about Robert Burns, concerning his character, the nature and quality of his genius, and his place in the world of literature.

This, however, remains undisputed and indisputable: he is the first great poet of the common people; meaning thereby, not merely that he is the first great poet to emerge from the common people, but the first who has found in them his continual theme and the source of his inspiration. Therein rests the assurance of his permanent place among the world's immortal singers; for the future belongs to the common people. But while his position as the poet of the common people has been taken for granted, its significance as a means of estimating thc value of his service to humanity has been almost wholly lost sight of by his numerous commentators, critics, and worshippers, who, in their desire to *place* him comparatively with other poets and men of letters, have failed to give proportionate consideration to his value as a *force* in the shaping of the thought of humanity, and consequently in the directing of human affairs. The trend towards democracy during the last hundred years owes more to Robert Burns than has yet been conceded in any estimate of his character and work.

This tendency to overlook and ignore Burns' chief characteristic found its most notable illustration in the late Mr. Henley's famous, or at least notorious essay, and also in the nature of the criticisms evoked by that brilliant but lop-sided performance. Quite a flood of invective ensued, mostly from perfervid Scottish patriots, and directed chiefly against the essayist's slightly brutal references to the poet's personal failings rather than to the main argument whereby Henley, in the very act of paying homage to the Scottish poet's genius, sought to classify him as a poetical back-number, a kind of glorious antique, whose influence upon modern thought was to all intents and purposes a negligible quantity.

The incensed enthusiasts, in their zeal for the character of their hero, flew off at a tangent, leaving the main issue practically untouched, and proving that they, equally with their adversary, had not even begun to appreciate the true nature of Burns' service to humanity, which consists not only in that he was a great Scottish poet, but in the fact that he was a great poet with a new message. Henley and his critics alike were concerned with the medium of the message rather than with the message itself. They failed to look for that which Carlyle had desiderated concerning Burns seventy years previously—a true standard "whereby to estimate what he really was and did in the eighteenth century for his country and the world."

Henley's theory is that Burns was the last (and of course the greatest) of the old Scots school of poets; a theory which may be undeniably true, and yet leave the essential truth unspoken. He contrives to make his theory seem convincing, and almost scientific, by setting it up against another imaginary theory which is even more misleading. Here is the theory, as elaborated in the preface to the centenary edition. I quote it in full, as it helps me in the way I want to go.

"Burns," says Henley, "for all his exhibition of some modern tendencies, was not the founder of a dynasty, but the heir of a flourishing tradition, and *the last of an ancient line;* he is demonstrably the outcome of an environment, and not in any but the narrowest sense the unnatural birth of Poesy and Time, which he is sometimes held to be. Being a great artist, he derives from a numerous ancestry; and like all great artists, he is partly an effect of local and peculiar conditions, and partly the product of immediate and remote forebears. Genius apart, in fact, he is *ultimus Scotorum,* the last expression of the old Scots world, and therewith the culmination of a school deep-rooted in the past, which by producing such men as Dunbar and Scott, and Alexander Montgomery; as Ramsay and Fergusson, and the nameless lyrists of the song-books, made it possible for him to be."

Thus is Burns safely deposited amongst the ancients and securely barred out from amongst the moderns, of whom he was the forerunner; from the company of the poets of freedom—Shelley and Byron and Wordsworth and Longfellow and Whitman and Swinburne. "Burns was of us," said Browning; but W. E. Henley thought otherwise, and maintained his conclusions, as we see, most learnedly and plausibly. We can almost see Burns in the making, and especially in the ending; deriving from his numerous ancestry and ending as *"ultimus Scotorum,* the last expression of the old Scots world." "Hc is demonstrably the outcome of an environment." Who will deny it of Burns, or of any other? We are all the outcome of an environment, not the great artists only but the obscure dullards and nobodies, and all this learned theorising does not take us very far, either in accounting for Robert Burns or in estimating his work, least of all in measuring the *effect* of his work.

Henley, of course, does not apply his pseudo-determinism literally and scientifically. To do that he would have had to trace the genealogy of the peasant man and woman from whom Burns sprang, and that would have been no easy task—beyond a certain not very remote point, quite impossible—though along that line of enquiry there might have been found the sources of some at least of those transmitted mental characteristics which specially distinguished him, and in their combination constitute what we call the genius of Burns. That grandsire who was out in the '45, and that other relative on the maternal side who died at Aird's Moss fighting for religious liberty, had probably a greater share in the mental make-up of this imaginative, patriotic, and liberty-loving peasant-poet than all his literary predecessors.

It is not, however, the poet's lineal ancestry that is called to witness, but his literary ancestry; certain Scottish poets from whom Burns learned some of his poetic craftsmanship, but whose work, it should be noted, was available to others than Burns, and to some of them in a much greater degree than it could ever have been to this working ploughman.

Henley's contribution to Scottish literary history is valuable, doubtless, but it does not account for Robert Burns. It helps to explain why, Robert Burns being there, he of necessity worked through certain stereotyped methods of expression, but it does not account for the nature of the expression, for the thing expressed. And it does not explain why this numerous literary ancestry should have culminated in this particular Scottish peasant, and not in another; in Robert, for example, and not in Gilbert. No theory that I have heard of can explain that. Henley himself seems to recognise this, and leaves a way out which sets his whole theory on one side.

"Genius apart, he is *ultimus Scotorum."* But genius apart there would have been no Burns the poet. There would only have been Burns the ploughman, who would have had no use for the literary ancestry; and we should not to-day be discussing the why and the wherefore of him. On the whole, when we come to look at the matter closely, Henley simply rehabilitates the theory he set out to destroy, the theory that Burns *is* the unnatural birth of Poesy and Time, which is a sorry end to a painstaking argument, and is of course absurd.

Certainly, the conclusion that Burns is merely the last of an ancient line is altogether untenable in view of the fact that to-day, after one hundred years, his appeal is still to that element in humanity which looks *forward* rather than backward. Walter Scott, who came later, is more antiquarian, not to say antiquated, both in spirit and outlook than Robert Burns. It is not true even to say that he was the last of the Scottish vernacular school of poetry. The greatest certainly, but not the last. There has probably been more vernacular verse written since his time than before it, some of it of a kind that would rank very high had it not to bear comparison with the supreme glory of Burns himself, who stands towards it as the great exemplar. I call to mind "Kilmeny" and some of the songs of Lady Nairne as examples that will compare not unfavourably with the best of the Scots vernacular poetry anterior to Burns.

When we are told that Burns was the last expression of the old Scots world, we naturally ask, "Which old Scots world?" For there have been more than one, and there were more than one comprised in the period of time covered by the poetic pedigree cited by Henley. Dunbar, the greatest of our Scottish poets prior to Burns, and the only one comparable to him in point of genius, was a begging Franciscan friar, and later a court dependant; Henryson, who preceded him, was a schoolmaster who taught his scholars within the precincts of a still flourishing abbey and beneath the shadow of a royal palace wherein the Scottish king still held his court. Their world was a Catholic world—semi-scholarly, semi-barbarous, mediaeval and feudalistic. Burns could not be said to be the last expression of *that* old Scots world. The Reformation had made an end of it.

Scott and Montgomery belonged to the turbulent time immediately following the Reformation, when it was still a question of doubt whether the new or the old forms of religion would mould the thoughts and dominate the life of the Scottish people—a time in which art of any kind found small opportunity for expression. With *that* old Scots world Burns had nothing in common. From these elder "makkars," so far as he was conversant with them—which was not very far—he borrowed some of his rhythms and measures, but nothing of his poetic outlook. He was born into a Protestant, Calvinistic world, as different from theirs as the twentieth century is from the eighteenth. Ramsay and Fergusson were also of that later world; but of their verse the most that can be said is that it was symptomatic of the reaction against the too strait-laced puritanism superimposed by Calvinistic theology upon the social life of the Scottish people.

From them Burns took nothing but the stimulus of their example. He was too close to reality to be misled by the romantic gentle shepherds of Allan Ramsay; while the more original Fergusson, dying before he had rightly begun to live, had no great legacy to pass on to his great successor. Burns paid homage to both, especially Fergusson, recognising in his fate some affinity with his own. But he looked upon that old Scots world quite differently from them: from the standpoint of the peasant, and with the eye of genius. Where they saw only the surface and fringes of society he saw it comprehensively, and discovered what neither poet nor historian had yet discovered—the importance of the common people.

To the suggestion that what Henley meant was that Burns is the last expression of Scottish life and character before it became absorbed and merged in the life and character of the English people, there is the plain answer that *the absorption has not yet taken place,* after a hundred years' opportunity for assimilation. Scottish life and character has changed in consonance with modern industrial environment, but it has not become English life and character.

Nationality has a habit of persisting. It derives some of its most vital characteristics from the natural features of the country in which it has been nourished; and although it is true that modern industrial methods have a uniforming tendency temporarily destructive of individuality both in persons and nations, modern industrialism has not yet laid low the Scottish hills, nor softened the Scottish climate, nor taken the bloom off the heather. What it has done has been to take the people from the hills and from the land and place them in conditions where the assertion of character, national or personal, is more difficult than it was formerly. That, however, as all students of history know, is a passing phase. The Scottish people will get back to the Scottish land, and it will probably be found that not the least of the triumphs of the reorganised society of the future will consist in the restoration of communal individuality under permanently favourable conditions; thus providing fresh outlets for Art and Literature, and freeing them from that commercialist dominance in the midst of which they strive, even now with some measure of success, for natural expression.

Let it not be forgotten that once before Scottish literature was Anglicised almost out of existence, yet reasserted itself, the chief instrument in the revival being this same Robert Burns.

Given the right conditions, which are sure to come, it will do so again; and just as even now, in the midst of the alleged Anglo-Saxon ascendancy, there exists a distinctive Scottish School of Art, so also once again will there be a distinctive Scottish School of Literature, and the whole world will, as in the past, be the gainer thereby. And the renaissance, when it does arrive, will find itself debtor to Robert Burns. It will take its tune from the

Ayrshire peasant. For the future literary revival in Scotland and elsewhere must be, in the very nature of things, democratic. It must reflect the thoughts, passions, manners, and aspirations of the common people. Burns was the first amongst the poets to discover the common people, not merely objectively nor yet subjectively, as abstract material for the literary artist, but as the very source and foundation of inspiration. It might be better to say that Burns *revealed* the common people in his own personality and in his poetry, which in its every mood and phase is the expression of his personality. By virtue of that expression Burns holds his place, not only amongst the reminiscent singers of a world that is dead and buried, but amongst the great poets of the world to come.

A Man's a Man

It is not necessary to claim Burns as the founder of a dynasty. The realm of poesy indeed is, and has ever been, republican rather than dynastic; its gates wide open always, and its borders never so circumscribed by old tradition as to bar the way against newcomers with new ideals, or with new modes of expressing the old ideals.

Not the founder of a dynasty, but the pioneer of a new poetic enterprise. To speak of Burns as merely the heir to deep-rooted conventions is absurd. He brushed the old conventions aside. He made use of the old modes of expression, it is true, but he made use of them to express a new conception. Just as one might use an old earth-worn spade to dig up bright gold and shining diamonds; just as Columbus made use of an old-world ship to seek out a new world.

And yet the new world discovered by Burns was, as we have seen, a very old world. It was the world of the common people. "The merry, friendly country folks"; the "poor, oppressed, honest man"; the "toil-worn cottar"; the "buirdly chiels and clever hizzies"; in fact, all those ordinary, everyday folk upon whose "toils obscure an' a' that" depends, and has always depended, the entire fabric of society; in Burns' own phrase, "the simple hind, *whose toil upholds the glittering show.*"

They had been there from the beginning, these peasants, the basic element in Scottish national life. They were there through all the centuries, the burden-bearers, fechtin' men, and daily drudges, what time Henryson and Dunbar, and Scott and Montgomery, and David Lyndsay and Drummond of Hawthornden were weaving their poetic fancies and polishing their rhyming apostrophes. But the common people remained almost as invisible to these mediaeval poets and poetasters as they were, and are still, to the orthodox historian.

It needed a peasant-poet to see the peasant rightly. With Burns the people are not subsidiary; with him the people are all in all. It is the others who are subsidiary and parasitical; the belted knights and the struttin' birkies of lords, alike with the king their maker. For the first time these are placed in their right perspective, and the people step forward. This is a part of the real abiding service which Burns rendered to humanity; a service which will remain, even though—what is not likely—with the passing of the ages and the decay of the Scottish doric every scrap of his writings should find oblivion. He dignified, he elevated the common people. He saw them as no one else had ever seen them; as they had not even seen themselves, until he held up the mirror in which they were able for the first time to recognise their own importance, and were made thereby to become almost involuntarily socially conscious; what we to-day call class conscious.

I would not be misunderstood. Working-class life had been casually versified before Burns' time. I do not forget "Christ's Kirk on the Green," nor "Habbie Simpson," nor "Maggie Lauder." I do not forget the "nameless lyrists of the song-books," nor the unknown folk-singers whose rough-and-ready reflections of incidental phases of working-class life it was part of Burns' work to transfigure and purify; and I would be no true Scot if I sought to depreciate the value of their services in keeping alive the flickering flame of Scottish song in the hearts of the people in the days of their serfdom. But that is the full extent of their services. They are episodal, fragmentary. Not one, nor all of them, present a comprehensive picture of working-class life, or reveal the spirit of the common people. And they do not uplift nor inspire. The common people, so far as they speak for themselves, or are spoken for, in song and ballad, are still quite contentedly the lower classes, the serfs and hinds and menials. Burns completely changed the point of view. With him there enters into the literature of the people a note of self-respect; nay, more, a note of exaltation. He was the first to say, "A man's a man for 'a that!" He said it not in one song only, but in many songs. In his satires against Calvinism not less than in his sarcasms against pride of place and privilege; in his lamentations for human suffering not less than in his songs of the joy of life. The thought itself, embodying the principle of natural equality irrespective of rank or caste or material possessions, was not an entirely new thought. For a generation at least it had been permeating the mind of Europe, silently sapping and mining at the foundations of feudalism. It found philosophic expression in the writings of Rousseau, and was the moving principle behind the French Revolution. Paine in his "Rights of Man" familiarised it to the English-speaking race, and it managed to get itself embedded in the constitution of the new American republic, where, cynics say, it has remained stowed away safe and harmless ever since; an interment due to the growth of new social distinctions created by capitalistic developments which neither Rousseau, nor Tom Paine, nor Washington could foresee, developments which make the affirmation of the principle as necessary to-day as it was a hundred years ago. But till Burns came, the new idea had not found its poet. He was the first to give it utterance in song, that method of appeal which most convincingly reaches the mind of the common people. His was no last minstrel's lay sighing over declining feudalistic glories. It was a forerunner's song heralding the coming of the common people, and has been echoed and re-echoed by nearly every great singer since his day. It has been carried round the world by the emigrating and colonising Scottish peasantry, and enters into the very fibres of the new overseas democracies. "A man's a man!" With the striking of this note the common people began to take their rightful place in literature and in the world. Their enfranchisement had begun, though parliament had to wait a hundred years for the tread of their footsteps. In one day, in the mere lilt of a song, so to speak, democracy leapt forward. Democracy in Scotland asserted itself, not with a vote, nor with a sword, but with a song; and whether in its final vindication democracy shall use the vote or the sword, behind the weapon and the blow will be the song of Robert Burns. Ere the theory of Socialism had begun to shape itself, the claim of Socialism had found a voice. For what is the claim of Socialism but this—that the conditions shall prevail wherein manhood shall have free play, wherein a man shall be a man? This was Burns' message to humanity. He was the first great poet to deliver that message; and the fact that despite the limitations of his medium of expression he was able to command the world's attention, stamps him for ever as one of the world's men of power. His medium was the vernacular, the hamely, auld Scots doric; a form of speech familiar only to a small corner of the British dominions, a language, as some say, uncouth and obscure, well-nigh obsolete, and, when Burns appeared, ready to be swept away by the rising Anglo-Saxon flood. It was good enough for Burns and his message. The old Scots doric was to him as an ancient harp might be to a minstrel of genius, who from the thumb-worn strings awakens a great new heart-stirring melody. Burns' new melody on the old Scottish harp reaches to the heart of humanity, and places him among the poets who are more than local and more than national, who are universal and for all time. For while there is no poet who is so truly in the literal sense of the term a national poet, yet there is none who has done so much as he to break down national boundaries and destroy racial antipathies. The common people are the common people in all lands. A man's a man, or ought to be, everywhere.

This poetic promulgation of the idea of natural human rights was all the more notable because of the time and the place and the circumstances in which it found utterance. All the conditions in Scotland, political, social, and ecclesiastical, were such as to stifle the very idea of independence. Politically, Scotland had sunk into a mere appendage of England; and Burns' malediction—

> Lord, send a rough-shod troop o' hell,
> O'er a' wad Scotland buy and sell!

was already well earned. Her government was simply a corrupt bureaucracy manipulated in the interests of a few territorial families. Her industrial system was no more than a kind of bastard feudalism with the overlordship responsibilities left out. Her religious life had degenerated from the democratic conception of Knox into superstitious formalism.

It was Burns who said, "Facts are chiels that winna ding, and daurna be disputed." Yet his whole work, his life, he himself, what were they but protests against existing facts—against the dominant facts of the society in which he was placed? The fact of ecclesiastical authority controlling men's beliefs; the facts of kingly, or aristocratic, or plutocratic authority controlling men's actions. He disputed the facts all along the line, and "dang" them to some tune, though he himself ultimately went down in the conflict. And there was one tremendous fact involved in all these others, the rightfulness of which he disputed all through life, and with his latest breath: the fact of poverty—the poverty of the common people.

He had no illusions concerning the world in which he lived, this peasant. He was no dreamy mystic, nor yet romanticist. Idealist he was, as all poets are, but he was also realist, as many poets are not. Occasional glances he cast backward into the romance of a lost cause, as of the Stuarts; but concerning the actual world in which he lived he had no misconceptions. He was too near to reality—

> . . . Nurst in the Peasant's lowly shed,
> To hardy Independence bravely bred,
> By early Poverty to hardship steeled,
> And trained to arms in stern Misfortune's field.

The son of a "toil-worn cottar," he himself toil-worn and not a little care-scarred, even ere he had emerged from childhood, he knew, and never ceased to know, that his fate was the fate of all his social compeers. He was born in poverty, he lived in poverty, and he died in poverty. That was, and is, the fate of the common people. Burns' attitude towards that fate was never acquiescence, but rebellion always. He never accepted poverty for justice. He accepted it for what it was and is—injustice. "Why should a'e man better fare, an' a' men brithers?" Even in his most philosophical and kindliest mood he enters his protest—

> It's hardly in a body's pow'r
> To keep at times frae being sour
> To see how things are shared.
> How best o' chiels are whyles in want,
> While coofs on coontless thousands rant
> An kenna how to ware't.

The modern apologists for things as they are, who from time to time seek to ordain Burns in the popular mind as a kind of high priest of the gospel of content, are guilty of the worst kind of perversion. The puritans who sermonise over his social failings never did worse than that. They have some basis for their sermons. The others have none for their misdirected eulogiums. Burns loved to "tak' aff his dram," and he "dearly lo'ed the lasses," and sometimes he gave his muse a loose rein down pleasure's more disreputable byways—practices all of them antipathetic to the "unco guid"; but he was no apostle of social contentment. He was, as every rebel must be, a discontented man. And in this, as in most other aspects of his character, he was typical. His discontent was the expression of the justifiable discontent of his class, the common people. It is true that he reflected also the brave optimism of labouring folk, who even out of the hardest environment contrive for themselves a little happiness. The natural gaiety of the man, his loving kindness, and his ever present sense of humour reveal themselves in his intensely sympathetic descriptions of the simple pleasures of peasant life; but ever and anon he flames out in wrath and rage against the injustice of the peasant's fate, or melts into tears of pity for the hard, unlovely lot of the poor. That the life of the eighteenth-century Scottish peasant was not utterly joyless is true, just as it is true to-day that the inhabitant of the city slum can catch an occasional glimpse of the sun. But neither the peasant's transient joys nor the slum-dweller's stolen sunshine justify contentment. They rather, because of their evanescence and precariousness, intensify the sense of wrong. Of the transitory pleasures of the Scottish peasantry no one has given so vivid impressions as Burns. Their Hallowe'en feasts and Fasten-e'en rockins; their kirns and weddings and New Year social gatherings; their domestic felicities—

> The canty auld folks, crackin' croose,
> The young anes rantin' through the hoose ;

their John Barleycorn joys, and the joys of love, lawful

and illicit; all the intermittent relaxations with which the labour-weary peasants sought to beguile the "kiaugh and care" of their daily lives—they are all to be found in the pages of Burns, and remain a priceless possession, illuminative at once of the social habits of the people and of the unconquerable vitality of the Scottish race. But these are fitful joys, snatched from a dreary environment of harassing care and toil and trouble; they are the bright spots in a picture lit up by the genius and humour of Burns, but a picture whose shadows are deep and sombre, and whose background is poverty. "The Cottar's Saturday Night" presents a pleasant, restful, almost idyllic grouping, but it is a "toil-worn" man who sits at the head of the table; the "priest-like father" trudged "weary o'er the moors" only an hour ago, and his "spade, his mattocks, and his hoes" are truer emblems of his daily life than is the "big ha'-Bible." They are happy enough peasant folk who gather round the fire on that "merry day the year begins." They deserve to be, for all the rest of the year it has been their lot to "drudge and drive through wet and dry," "howkin' in sheuchs" and "biggin' dykes wi' dirty stanes," getting rheumatism in their bones, and growing old before their time. Too old at forty is hardly an exclusively twentieth-century grievance. Listen to Burns, and, while you admire his handling of the doric, realise the tragedy of the life of the common people—

> For, ance that five-and-forty's speel'd,
> See crazy, weary, joyless eild,
>   Wi' wrinkled face,
> Comes hostin', hirplin' owre the field
>   Wi' creepin' pace.

This is no mere poetic figure. It is grim realism. Burns saw it exemplified in his own father, who was prematurely beaten into his grave by toil and care and poverty.

The background of Burns' picture of Scottish peasant

life is poverty. In the picture there is love and laughter, and dram-drinking, and high spirits in plenty, but at the back of it all, beclouding it all, there is poverty. And not only material poverty, but spiritual, or shall we say unspiritual, poverty? There are not only the humiliated, "poor tenant bodies, tholin' the factor's snash"; not only the

> Poor o'er-laboured wight, so abject, mean and vile,
> Begging a brother of the earth to give him leave to toil;

not only "age and want, that ill-matched pair," symbolical of the utter hopelessness of the labourer's lot; but side by side with these there are the "Ayr Presbyters" and the "Holy Fairs," and the "Holy Willies," with their "three-mile prayers and half-mile graces," with their narrow spiritual outlook, their intolerance and bigotry, and all the spirit-cramping, soul-destroying tyranny of hide-bound creeds and ignorant superstitions which held the common people in mental fetters, and over a whole nation seemed to give the lie to the assertion that "a man's a man." It is the picture of a people laird-ridden and priest-ridden, held, in fact, in a double bond of poverty, material and mental. And it was from the midst of this environment that Burns sent his message to the world, "A Man's a Man for a' that!"

Brotherhood

Robert Burns was in rebellion against both kinds of poverty. That is not to say that he set himself deliberately to wage war against the forces that create poverty. Burns was not a man of deliberation, except towards the end of his life. Had he been, it might have been better for himself, though the worse for the world's poetic heritage. He never sought out the enemy in the gate. There was no need. The enemy sought him out. Poverty found him where the muse found him, at the plough. Perhaps it might be truer to say that poverty placed him there. Burns was in rebellion instinctively, and the nature of his revolt was determined by the circumstances of his immediate environment. He was girt round about by the visible effects of poverty, material and mental. To effectively fight the former was impossible. To escape from it was equally impossible. But mental poverty—the repression of mind and spirit—to fight that was not only possible, it was unavoidable to a man like Burns. Gifted with the power of satirical expression to a degree vouchsafed to no other man before or since, he found himself, just when his genius was ripening to activity, in his Ayrshire parish, right in the heart of what ultimately, and very largely through his intervention, developed into a nation-wide conflict between authority and rationalism in religion. There was only one possible side for Robert Burns. He was for liberty always. He took his side, not deliberately, but because he could do naught else. It was his nature to. It must be remembered, what usually is forgotten, that he chose the unpopular side; the side which, superficially looked at, was opposed to the rights of the people. It was only through his influence that it ultimately became popular. The common people of Scotland were not burning with zeal for religious liberty.

They had no desire to be set free from the thraldom of creeds. Their personal devil had become to them a kind of necessity; and they saw nothing wrong with a God who sent "ane to heaven and ten to hell" for His own glory. It was not the people who were demanding a more liberal theology. It was, strange though it may seem, certain liberal-minded church patrons who were thrusting new theologians upon narrow-minded and unwilling presbyteries and congregations. Burns was on the side of the liberal-minded patrons and the new theologians. That is to say, he *appeared* to be against the people. The people had to be set free, not from corrupt church government, but first of all from the slavery of their own minds.

This was Burns' achievement, not deliberately undertaken, but in the assertion of his own mental freedom. One thing the common people of Scotland had never lost amidst all their abasement. They still retained their sense of humour. And Burns' humour, bitter and kindly by turns, directed against their ingrained beliefs, caught them where they were most vulnerable. It appealed, as all true humour ever does, to their common sense. A pretty parochial squabble it seemed; an affair of presbyteries, and kirk-sessions and patrons, intermingled with personal rancours and spites; a parish pump affair, one would have said, had not Robert Burns been there. But Robert Burns being there made all the difference. His satires—not even meant to be printed—against the Presbytery of Ayr and all the little crowd of heresy-hunters struck at the very heart of religious intolerance everywhere. Bigotry was put upon its defence, and this was the kind of attack to which bigotry is unaccustomed. The appeal was, as I have said, not to authority, or precedent, or metaphysics, but to common sense. "Curst common sense, that imp o' hell," as the other side naturally regarded it, and as Burns phrased it for them.

In half-a-dozen poems, written in the leisure moments of a working farmer's life, more was done for the intellectual liberation of the Scottish people than has been accomplished by the entire army of higher critics since that time. The higher criticism, indeed, is largely the outcome of Burns' attack, and in some of its aspects is little more than a soothing apologetic, intended to dull the edge of the Ayrshire peasants' weapons. The particular phase of the quarrel which brought Burns into the fray has long since disappeared. But the main quarrel, between authority and reason, between bigotry and common sense, is raging still; and the Scottish peasant-poet is still in the front of the battle.

Thus it was fated that this son of genius, whose own personal and ever-present quarrel was with material poverty, should deliver his first strong blows against mental poverty, the poverty which enslaves the mind. That, as I say, was a matter of circumstance. Had he been born and bred in another part of the west of Scotland, amongst the weavers of Glasgow, for example, or had he lived longer, who can doubt that his genius would have been at the service of the Reform movement, which was then struggling into existence? And who can doubt that in that case we should have had from him more than the one or two casual references to Muir and Palmer, the Reform martyrs. Almost certainly he would himself have been amongst the martyrs. As it is, his influence on that side of the progressive movement is greater than can be measured. The struggle for political freedom was simply the materialistic counterpart of the free-thought conflict; differing only in that its basis was economic rather than spiritual, its purpose social rather than religious.

In essence the two movements were, and are, one and the same; seeking always to establish liberty for body and soul. Whoever was fighting in the one was helping the other.

Burns was in both. He was against oppression, whether the instrument was the priest or the laird, the presbytery or the Government; whether the source of authority was Kirk or State, Calvinism or feudalism; fighting in the only way possible for him, not with the weapons of the agitators or the politicians, but with the weapons of the poet; and doing this, not deliberately and with calculation, but incidentally, instinctively, and impulsively. The case for the people as against caste, and wealth, and privilege has never been stated more powerfully than by Robert Burns. In two poems, widely differentiated from each other in style and artistry, he has probed to its very core the disease of modern society. "The Twa Dogs" and "Man was made to Mourn" express the whole of Burns' social philosophy. They also embody the whole of the present-day indictment, economic and moral, against society. "Man was made to Mourn" is at once a lamentation and a protestation, a song of tears and, if we would read it aright, a call to arms. They pervert the very spirit of the poem who find in it a fatalistic acceptation of universal doom, an embittered version of the Hebrew preacher's "Vanity of vanities!" Burns did not believe that man is *born* to trouble "as the sparks fly upward," that the purpose of man's being is sorrow. He did not believe that "man was made to mourn." Was not he the optimistic singer of universal brotherhood? He believed that man was made to rejoice, and that if he was prevented from realising his natural heritage of joy, it was because of conditions which man himself had created and would change. The dirge-like monotone, reiterant of what sounds like a chant of despair, is not the acceptation of the everlasting inevitability of human suffering. It is a grave and solemn statement, austere in its simplicity, of social facts, as they exist, as they ought not to exist, and as they need not exist. The doctrine of necessitarianism, as implying the permanence of injustice on earth, was as revolting to Burns as the doctrine of hell-fire hereafter.

He questioned the necessity for human wrong as emphatically as he questioned the necessity for Divine wrath. If injustice and wrong are inevitable, designed from all eternity to all eternity, why was the heaven-erected face of man adorned with the smiles of love? Why was an independent wish implanted in the human mind? Man's nature cries out against it, and Burns, in the very act of describing the effects of social injustice, voices humanity's protest; the same protest which is on the lips of the workless man to-day, and puts power into the Socialist movement the wide world over. It is the same protest to which he gives utterance in another way in "The Twa Dogs." Brimful of humour, and of inimitable characterisation both of dogs and men, this poem is a veritable chapter of social history, a revelation of the life of the common people in the eighteenth century, and also of the other people whose life was that of the parasite; types who, differentiated only by changing fashion and industrial variation, are to be found in every society organised on the principle of production for profit. These two poems, wide apart as they are in point of style and colour—the one sombre and serious, the other humorous and serious—have this common characteristic, that while laying bare human follies arising out of social injustice they are free from class bitterness. They do not inspire to hatred. It is humanity that suffers, and it is humanity that is to blame, if blame there be. In "The Twa Dogs" especially there is a great and kindly human tolerance,

> For thae frank, rantin', ramblin' billies,
> Fient haet o' them's ill-hearted fellows.

Yet it is these same frank, rantin', ramblin' billies whose

social conduct gives force to the impeachment that "Man's inhumanity to man makes countless thousands mourn."

It is as if Burns had anticipated the modern Socialist maxim, "not the individual but the system." Rich and poor are alike demoralised by the foolish and unjust social arrangements. The poor, the common people, suffer most; they suffer all the time; but the wrong is humanity's. In brotherhood, and in brotherhood only, lies the means of righting the wrong. That was Burns' ideal.

It is not suggested that he had visualised to his own mind the new social order which would give reality to his ideal of brotherhood. We are speaking, not of a political economist, but of a poet, and of a poet whose life, involving a never-ceasing struggle merely to maintain a footing upon mother earth, precluded all opportunity—even supposing he had possessed the necessary temperament, and the times had been ripe—for that scientific inquiry into social problems which even the political economists had hardly begun. But the fundamental facts which are the basis of that inquiry were well known to Burns. Too well known. We know that in the later years of his life he had read at least twice over Adam Smith's "Wealth of Nations," borrowed from his friend, Graham of Fintry. He did not, however, require Adam Smith to explain to him that riches and poverty are correlated as cause and effect. That was one of the lessons he had been learning from his infancy in the hardest of schools. Nor did he require Adam Smith to prove to him that labour is the source of wealth. He had himself stated this, both in his poems and in his letters. The following passage from one of his letters to Mrs. Dunlop is a definite and clear statement of the relations between labour and capital, and would fall quite naturally from the lips of any twentieth-century Socialist: "'Tis now about the term day, and there has been a revolution among those creatures who, though in appearance partakers, and equally noble partakers of the same nature with Madame, are from time to time—their nerves, their sinews, their health, strength, wisdom, experience, genius, time, nay, a good part of their very thoughts—sold for months and years, not only to the necessities, the conveniences, but the caprices of the important few;" and to Mr. Peter Hill he wrote, "I do not think that avarice of the good things we have is born with us; but we are placed here amid so much nakedness and hunger, and poverty and want, that we are under a damning necessity of studying selfishness, in order that we may exist."

There is plenty of evidence to show that he had a clear perception of the economic cause of poverty, and also a conception, if not of the actual remedial processes, certainly of the principle upon which those processes must be based. Professor Dugald Stewart expressed surprise that Burns had formed some conception of the "doctrine of association," a surprise which illustrates naively the aloofness of the academic mind. The doctrine of association, whether of ideas or persons, is simply the philosophical formula for the poetic ideal which the wide world over is linked with the name of Robert Burns. In that ideal is embodied the principle of all social progress. For if brotherhood be the ideal, it is also, though it seems a paradox, the means towards the ideal. Only by brotherhood can brotherhood be established. It is impossible to conceive of any other way. In the beginning it may be a brotherhood of defence, as of the family, or of the clan; but in the end it must be a brotherhood of love. That is the poet's conception. The "doctrine of association," says the philosopher. "Organisation and co-operation," says the Socialist. "Brotherhood," says the poet. It is the business of the Socialist to give effect to the poet's ideal; and it is very doubtful if this great principle could have got itself so widely spread and so deeply rooted in the hearts of men if this Robert Burns had not been there in the eighteenth century to give it utterance in such a way as to appeal to the mind of the common people. In the directness and simplicity of the appeal lies its strength and power. "It's comin' yet, for a' that!" Faith and confidence are more than half the battle. The fact that these words have been singing round the world for a hundred years is worth more to the cause of human progress than whole libraries of philosophy. They are, in truth, the sum of all true social philosophies.

Burns the Rebel

That this man, to whose nature liberty was as the very breath of life, should, when the time came, find himself in active sympathy with the French Revolution and with the American Revolution was inevitable; just as inevitable as that the present-day British Socialist should find himself in sympathy with the revolutionists of Russia, with the educationists of Spain, and with the movements for self-government in Ireland and India. And it was just as natural that the authorities of his time should seek to repress and suppress Robert Burns as it is that the government of to-day should misrepresent and if possible suppress Socialist sympathy with these latter movements. The analogy should not be lost sight of either by Socialists or by the critics of Socialists.

The Reform associations and corresponding societies stood relatively in much the same position towards the ruling powers as do the Socialist organisations of to-day. And just as history has justified the former, so will it justify the latter. Burns' biographers have, I think without exception, chosen to adopt a tone of apology concerning his attitude at this period of his life, as if his outspokenness were some kind of lapse from common sense, a foolish, irresponsible indiscretion, excusable in a man like Burns, but highly regrettable.

There is no ground for such a view. Burns' attitude was entirely consistent with his past life, with his own nature, and with the spirit of his poetic work. The same impulse which in the earlier Mauchline days threw him on the side of the religious reformers, in the Dumfries period threw him on the side of the revolutionists. Had he failed to choose his side, and to choose the right side, he would have been recreant to those very principles of liberty of which his genius has made him, in literature at least, one of the chief protagonists. He could do naught else. It was the common people who had risen, and he was one of them. His sympathy with the revolutionists was the proof that whatever modification of outlook had come to him in his brief passage through the world of wealth and fashion, his belief in freedom and his love for the common people had remained steadfast, uncorrupt and incorruptible. The Burns who wrote the "Ode to Liberty," the "Welcome to Despots," and the "Ballad on the American War," was the same Burns who wrote the "Holy Fair" and "The Ordination."

But there was a difference. Some of the power had gone out of him. His faith in freedom was undimmed, but he himself had lost some of his freedom. And he had lost it even through the very means he had taken to secure it. It was to secure his own personal independence that he took service in the Excise. To "mak' siccar" at least against the extreme rigours of poverty for his wife and family, and thereby hold himself free in his hours of leisure to follow the muse without fear or favour: that was why Robert Burns became a gauger. And this that was meant for the rock of his independence became as a rock of serfdom to which he was chained. Every word spoken in sympathy with Washington and the American patriots, every word spoken in sympathy with the common people in France was a word spoken against the British Government, his employers, who held control of his material destinies. Had he been worldly wise and a time-server, as some of his commentators seem to think he ought to have been, he would have remained silent. That was impossible for Robert Burns. So he spoke out, and there was probably more moral courage in the speaking out than he has ever received credit for. In the early days when he struck out against bigotry he was unknown, and his public was only a small Ayrshire parish. Now he was well known and famous, and his audience was the whole nation. He knew this quite well. And he knew also that the nation, officially through its Government and through its governing classes, was opposed to the opinions which he felt bound to express.

Yet there can be no doubt that the knowledge of the possible consequences to his family, the thought of what the loss of his one meagre source of income would mean to them, limited and curbed the force of his expression. And when the official coercion was applied—as it was bound to be—he made his submission, and democracy's greatest voice was stifled at the moment when democracy had most need of it. That, to me, is the real tragedy of Robert Burns. In his soul he was humiliated and he was a proud man this peasant.

"Burns was a poor man by birth and an exciseman by necessity; but—I will say it—the sterling of his honest worth no poverty could debase, and his independent British mind oppression might bend, but it could not subdue." Thus he wrote to John Francis Erskine, under stress of the occasion, and in anticipation of posterity's verdict.

The situation could not be better described. He was bent, but not broken. And the bending of Robert Burns must have meant for him a process of mental conflict which one would rather not think of. Nevertheless, he left no room for doubt, either to his contemporaries or to posterity, as to his attitude towards those great events which were convulsing Europe and laying the foundations of a new nation in America. In these days all kinds of pretenders seek to associate themselves with the name of Robert Burns; but no defender of class privilege, no opponent of liberty, no traitor to democracy has a right to claim that Robert Burns is on his side.

Not the least bitter element in the situation was the fact that his country, Scotland, the land he loved, was through its governing classes suborned to the cause of the oppressor. He was, in his blood and marrow, a patriot. Love of country was like a religion to him. It was his daily theme. But his patriotism was no narrow, selfish creed. Love of country with him was simply love of liberty expressed in the terms of nationalism. A country enslaved was a country to be made free. And it was this beloved country of his, his "auld respectit mither," the land whose greatest glory it was that it had stood among nations for the principle of independence. It was this dear land that, in the same hour

> Which saw the generous English name
> Link't with such damned deeds of everlasting shame,

was made to associate itself with the infamy and dishonour.

> Thee, Caledonia! Thy wild heaths among,
> Famed for the martial deed, the heaven-taught song,
> To thee I turn with swimming eyes!
> Where is that soul of Freedom fled?
> Immingled with the mighty dead
> Beneath that hallowed turf where Wallace lies.

Strange it is, that amid all the thousand annual orations to the memory of Burns the patriot, Burns the poet of brotherhood, Burns the nature-lover, there should seem to be a common conspiracy to becloud and hide the figure of Burns the rebel.

We know, and Burns knew, that the common people, both in England and Scotland, were guiltless of the crimes against liberty committed by their governments —that they, in fact, were amongst the sufferers from those same crimes; and that wherever possible, and by the only methods available, they were making their protest. They had on their own account the same quarrel with their governments as their compeers in Europe. Liberty was being throttled, and nowhere more ruthlessly than in Burns' own country, where packed juries and vindictively brutal judges were overriding even the not very tender existing laws, to intimidate the Reform leaders and terrorise the people. It was fated that Burns should never get into close touch with the Reform movement. By the time it had emerged convulsively from the embryonic stage his race was nearly run. While the Reform leaders were being transported to Botany Bay he was at hand-grips once more with poverty and with the unmistakable symptoms of deadly disease; precariously holding house and home together, and still writing immortal verse on fifty pounds a year, and even that being threatened. He had been even poorer than that in his time, in the years when his father had to fight the same heart-breaking battle.

> The piebald jacket let me patch once more,

he wrote to Graham of Fintry,

> *On eighteenpence a week I've lived before.*

But that heroic alternative was not possible now with a wife and family dependent upon him. And knowing what we know of Burns, of his nature, and of his life's record, we come to the conclusion that it was poverty, and that alone, that in the last years of his life lost Burns to the Reform movement.

The Might Have Been

Humanity has a heavy indictment against this evil which we call poverty. It is no mere idle speculation to say that the whole world was the loser through the poverty of Robert Burns. We may set aside the plea so often put forward, that the hard conditions of the peasant's lot were the natural nursing-ground for his particular kind of genius.

That theory may suit men like Lord Rosebery, who can look at poverty philosophically, from afar off; or men like Mr. Andrew Carnegie, who can look backwards and downwards upon poverty. It is not in accord with the laws of growth and development. The fruits of Burns' genius would have been greater had the material conditions of his life been better. Poverty never was good for man nor woman. The poverty-stricken man of genius is as an eagle with leaden-weighted pinions. He may soar high, but his flight is neither so lofty nor so far as it would have been without the fetters. Carlyle, himself peasant's son and man of genius, and to this day the one man who has looked with true sympathetic insight into the soul of this other peasant's son, speaking on this very aspect of the question, and with reference to Burns' father, says: "Had this William Burns' small seven acres of nursery-ground anywise prospered, the boy Robert had been sent to school, had struggled forward, as so many weaker men do, to some university, come forth not as a rustic wonder, but as a regular, well-trained, intellectual worker, and *changed the whole course of British literature*—for it lay in him to have done this." That is to say, had Burns' father been secure against poverty, his son Robert would have changed the whole course of British literature.

In these pages I have been arguing that even as it was he did that to some extent. He changed the outlook, and gave a new direction to the stream of poetic thought; nay, more, he changed the nature of the stream itself, giving it that democratic and humanitarian impulse and colour whose course and character can be traced through the whole of nineteenth-century literature, "as streams their channels deeper wear." But there can be no question that had his poverty been less, his powers would have been greater. Doubtless Carlyle was right. A university education would have been of great value to Robert Burns. We can judge of that by the heroic use which he made of the intermitting educational opportunities that came his way.

But deprivation of university training was not the worst turn that poverty did for Burns. It beset him at every step of his journey through life. And, especially at that supreme period of crisis when his whole future career depended upon what step he should take next, poverty drove him into a corner, and left him without an alternative between ruin and the patronage of the rich. Had not Burns been driven to desperate straits, the second edition of his poems would have been published, like his first, from Kilmarnock, and there would never have been any dedication to the noblemen and gentlemen of the Caledonian Hunt—those "distinguished members of the northern aristocracy," as Lockhart styles them—whose distinction would have died with them but for their accidental association with the ploughman. We are here, of course, in the region of the "might have been," but it is a reasonable conjecture that if the Edinburgh adventure could have been avoided, if Burns could have gone on steadily developing his powers at home in Ayrshire, maturing his genius in the same soil and atmosphere in which it had been nourished, his subsequent career, though less cometary and wayward, would have been quite as brilliant, and more satisfactory. The Edinburgh period was the least prolific, poetically, of his life, and its experiences and associations the least useful and stimulating. He himself was conscious of this, and after the first six months was sick of it, and looking for a way out, and for some secure anchorage from whence he could earn a competent living without hindrance to the free exercise of his poetic faculty. This was the one thing, apparently, which neither his literary patrons nor the northern aristocracy could give him. They did what they could in their well-meaning, condescending, patrician way. Let us give them all due credit and honour. Their help was necessary to Robert Burns at this juncture, and they gave it, some of them generously; but it was necessary only because of the poverty of Robert Burns. It is not the Edinburgh gentry I am indicting, but poverty. As he himself said later, when forced to take refuge in the Excise, "The question is not at what door of fortune's palace shall we enter in; but what doors does she open to us?" This was the only door that opened to him, and poverty drove him through it.

But our indictment against poverty in the case of Robert Burns goes much deeper, and it is not quite the same as Carlyle's. It is not that poverty withheld from him a university education, but that it withheld from him good health and length of days. Poverty killed him, as it has killed, and is killing daily, its tens of thousands of men and women of genius, and men and women of no genius.

The span of a man's life is threescore years and ten. Burns died at thirty-seven. He died at that age, not because he had lived fast, but because he had lived hard. It was not fast living nor deep drinking that killed Burns. It was overwork.

Poverty took him in his tender years and set him there in the Ayrshire fields behind the plough. Ere his limbs were grown, ere his bones were set, poverty asked him to do more than a grown man's work. It exposed him to the winter's cold, to the summer's heat, to the heavy "trauchlin' " toil in the ploughing-field, to the long day's darg in harvest time. Poverty sowed the seeds of disease in his body ere he had well begun to live. Poverty took him in his boyhood's days, and cast over his youthful shoulders a burden of care such as in a well-ordered society no human being, old or young, will be asked to carry. When William Burns stood, as no man should have to stand before another man, "tholin' the factor's snash," Robert, in spirit, stood with him, and the iron entered into his soul. It was of these things Burns died at thirty-seven.

Rheumatic fever, consumption; whatever the medical diagnosis, Burns died of poverty. I will be told that he was not alone; that many others have had a similar fate. I know. That is part of the case for Socialism. But at present we are speaking of Robert Burns and the loss to literature and to humanity through his early death. He came of good stock. He had behind him many generations of the open-air life. He ought to have lived long. We know the kind and the quantity of his literary output during the years in which he lived, but even that does not give us the measure of his possible output during the years in which he *ought to have lived.* He had only just passed from the years of receptivity. All that fine work of his was no more than his literary apprenticeship, work produced for the most part responsive to the casual events of every passing day: the quarrels of sectarians, the amours of lads and lasses, the carousals of beggars, the singing of birds, the murmuring of streams, the whistling of the winds and the howling of the storms, the shining day and the gloomy night. His work as we have it is the recording of passing impressions, impressions which his genius transformed into works of art, most of them imperishable. But, in the natural course of life, the days of high purpose and supreme achievement lay all before him, the days that never dawned; for poverty had killed him, and in killing him robbed the world of who shall say how much great poetic thought and noble inspiration.

There is no need to blame his contemporaries, the individual lairds, and factors, and government supervisors. They were, as we most of us are, but twigs on the social tree. Nor is there any need to indulge in retrospective pity for the man Robert Burns. We are not now considering Burns' loss, but humanity's loss. He, indeed, got more out of life than most men get. He got the love of women and the friendship of men, both of them in abundance. He got these because his nature would not be denied; because on the social and passional sides his nature was at once winning and masterful, and, in the very reaction from the too stern discipline of material poverty, demanded full measure of compensation, and got it while life lasted.

We are considering now the economic environments which conditioned his life and shortened it; not the influence of Bonnie Jean and Highland Mary, or of Willie Nicol and the barley bree, but of the heavy toil, and the high-rented land, and the hard bargain.

Quite a prosaic question this with which we are faced in Burns' life and death, but one which involves the future of poetry and art—the future, indeed, of civilisation. The question is—I am stating it crudely, I know—can social systems be much longer regarded as tolerable, which in their very nature hinder genius in every department from giving of its best? We have to sit in judgment upon ourselves collectively; upon society; and we have got to consider whether there is not now sufficient common sense in the world, or in our corner of it, to shape and mould a system of society which will not stone its prophets, nor make sport of its poets, nor starve its children, nor degrade its common people.

And this last is the most important, comprehending as it does all the others. For if it be true that the literature and art of the future must be democratic alike in its source and its tendencies, at once revealing and inspiring the life of the common people, then in proportion as that life is healthy, vigorous, and free, in the same proportion will literature and art be virile, original, and noble.

A Representative Man

It is with some fear and trembling I venture now to write concerning the poetic quality of Burns' work, concerning his place and value as inspired literary artist. It is of his power as a social force I have hitherto been writing, a power derived, of course, from his poetic force, and not separable therefrom, though it seems to me to have been so separated or altogether ignored by most of his commentators, even by those whose appreciation is most unrestrained. That, indeed, is my only apology for the writing of this book.

But of Burns the artist, of Burns the poet, how shall one hazard an opinion who is neither artist, nor poet, nor practised literary critic? I suppose it ought to be sufficient for me that he has been acclaimed as great poet and artist by other great poets and artists, and by all who are competent to judge of poetry and art. But it is not sufficient for me. I am not content merely to know that Shelley and Byron and Wordsworth and Browning, and Carlyle and Tennyson have all hailed him as a master. I want to know why he has charms for me, why he has charms for the common people. For it has to be acknowledged that while these others masters receive their homage almost exclusively from amongst that class—ever growing in numbers, let us hope—who love literature for literature's sake, Burns has won to himself the allegiance, not to say the affections, of great numbers who, outside of his sphere of influence, have little taste for literature. He holds the others too, it must be remembered, the cultured, book-learned people. His grip on the common folk is therefore not won by any debasement of the standard of literary workmanship, or by any sacrifice of artistic ideals. I want to know the secret of his power, and I want to know it, not from the literary critics, but at first hand if I can. Perhaps we shall get on the trail if we take Burns on that side where he is said to be most open to literary disparagement, where he is weakest rather than where he is strongest. "He has, moreover, little or no spirituality," says Walt Whitman in an estimate which, though appreciative, is curiously patronising in tone, coming from such a source. "He has, moreover, little or no spirituality. This last is his mortal flaw and defect, tried by highest standards." I suppose it is true; yet I call to mind Byron's retort upon his publisher: "You have so many '*divine*' poems—is it nothing to have written a *human* one?" We have so many poets of "spirituality"—is it nothing to have a poet of humanity? Therein, probably, lies some part of his affinity with the common people; for, if the truth must be told, the common people also have "little or no spirituality." They are flesh and blood. Their emotions are human emotions, not superhuman nor transcendental; pertaining to the world of which they know rather than to ethereal, imaginary worlds of which they do not know—the loves and hates, and fears and joys, and sorrows of common life, out of which are materialised tragedy and comedy, and laughter and tears, and song. These things may not be described as spirituality in the esoteric sense. Yet they are of the spirit: the spirit of humanity. Burns trod the solid earth, and never at any time had his head in the clouds, else he had been no poet of the common people. He was no ecstatic dreamer of dreams, losing himself in those realms of poesy whose atmosphere is part speculative philosophy and part mysticism. Earth and sea and sky, and the heart of man, these he saw vividly, nor sought to penetrate beyond:

Farewell, thou fair day, thou green earth, and ye skies,
Now gay with the bright setting sun;
Farewell, loves and friendships, ye dear, tender ties,
Our race of existence is run.

These four lines encompass Burns' entire poetic theme. Life and death, and their accessories. The world, and all that therein is. This world, his own small corner of it, held enough of beauty and pain and passion for him. He had no need—probably had not the power and inspiration—to build up fantastic other-worlds and fill them with imaginary pains and passions. Therein may lie, as Whitman says, "his mortal flaw and defect." Yet, may it not be that in that same "mortal flaw" rests the secret of his immortal fame, the "touch of nature" illumined with genius, which makes him kin to the common people for all time.

And there are compensations. Burns has that which is denied to some of the poets so richly endowed with spirituality, that which Whitman himself did not possess, or at least did not reveal; that which was granted to Chaucer and Shakespere and withheld from Shelley and Keats. He had humour. I have heard it conjectured that if to the intensity and lofty imagination of Shelley we could have had conjoined the humour of Burns, the result would have been a man of genius greater than Shakespere. That, of course, is mere hypothetical guess-work, which has no ending, and leads nowhere. But there can be no question that it is the possession of this faculty of humour by Burns, combined with his power of characterisation, which has led some not incompetent critics to classify his genius as Shakesperian.

I am making no such claim. I am merely claiming that we have here a more than adequate offset to the lack of spirituality. There are, indeed, experts in psychological hair-splitting who assert that humour itself is a kind of spirituality, and along that line of reasoning it might be maintained that "Tam o' Shanter" and "The Jolly Beggars" are quite as mentally stimulating as "Epipsychidion" and "Endymion."

For my present purpose these differentiations and comparisons do not matter. Burns is Burns, and Shelley is Shelley, and Keats is Keats. There is one glory of the sun and another of the stars, but which is which in the poetic firmament is for most of us determined by our point of view. I fancy that for the common people Burns is the sun, and these others are brilliant but rather coldy-shining stars; the reason being, that he is nearer to them. They can feel his warmth, and enjoy his light, and they and he have certain attributes in common, one of the chief of which is this sense or faculty of humour. The common people have not much leisure for dreaming dreams or seeing visions, but they can laugh, and they can make laughter. They can make laughter sometimes even out of their own miseries and misfortunes.

Burns did this, but he did more. He made laughter out of their most serious conventional beliefs, and revealed these beliefs for what they really were—superstitions. The humour of Burns when expressed in satire almost amounts to a kind of national introspection. The Scottish people laughed—and are laughing still—at the grotesque conception of religion as satirised by Burns, but when they found that they were laughing at themselves that grotesquerie was doomed. Burns did what the great poets of spirituality could not do, because they had no humour: he initiated a spiritual revolution. Milton made Satan a Titanic rebel; Burns made him a laughing-stock. Dante made Hades magnificently terrible; Burns abolished it. For who would be terrified by so familiar a fiend as "Auld Nickie-ben?" The everlasting fire lost its terrors when it became a "lowin' heugh," and with the removal of the "fear o' hell," clarity of vision in matters spiritual became possible. The humour of Burns was a freshening wind lifting the theological mists and fogs from the human mind, and thereby opening out new and wider spiritual horizons.

And it is withal a rare, versatile, catholic humour,

generous as well as sarcastic, kindly as well as caustic, fitting itself to all occasions and to every shade of character. Everywhere it "mak's itsel' at hame." At kirk or market, at the plough tail or at the smiddy fire, by the ingle-neuk or in the tavern. It smites like Burnewin's forehammer, and every stroke "comes on like death." It jags like a Scotch thistle, caresses like a mither's sang, or insinuates itself persuasively like a soft-blowing westlan' win'. It "dinner's wi' a lord," goes wooin' with peasant lads and lasses, has whimsical greetings for the world's newcomers, and hobnobs in "twa-handed crack" with the king of terrors himself.

And for all its free-flowing abandon—nay, because of that—we know it for the output of an artist, for the product of a conscientious craftsman who, even while he deprecatingly described his work as "stringin' blethers up in rhyme," took infinite pains with the workmanship and pride in the result. His style, vocabulary, rhymes and measures reflect his themes and moods. His medium and materials correspond to his purpose, which is surely the essential thing in art. The words "come skelpin', rank and file," the right, true, natural words as they might have fallen shrewdly from the lips of workaday men and women, and have all the effect of spontaneity; as involuntary as laughter itself, and as infectious.

This indeed is the impression produced by nearly all Burns' work—spontaneity, involuntariness, freshness. There may have been midnight oil, but you can never feel the smell of it. Instead there is the fragrance of the woods, the smell of the earth, and—let it be admitted quite freely—the aroma of Scotch whisky; but always natural simplicity of expression. It is this quality which makes him the most tuneful of all the lyrists. His melody is unforced. Like his humour it seems to come easily, naturally, as the song of a laverock, as the song of a mother to her bairn as the song of a lover to his lass.

That is really what Burns' songs are. They are not merely Burns' songs. They are the songs of birds and streams and mothers and lovers innumerable. They are musical and natural because they have their source in music and in nature. He has himself given away his secret most melodiously:

> On braes when we please then,
> We'll sit an' *sowth a tune;*
> Syne rhyme till't, we'll time till't,
> An' sing't when we hae dune.

Surely this is the natural way of the maker of songs. The "sowthing," lilting, or humming of tunes is the instinctive habit of all healthy human beings. Wherever you find a healthy man, woman, or child, there is a tune either on the lips or in the heart. The mother "sowths" or "croons" to her bairn, the workman to his task, the lover to his sweetheart, and the whole world of common folk "sowth" the tunes that have come to them, they know not how, like the air they breathe. This they did at least in the age of Robert Burns, until the factory system came and we had to get our tunes "sowthed" for us by machinery, by barrel-organs and gramophones. Burns sowthed and sowthed the old, old tunes which were the common heritage of the common people. The "mither tongue," the inspired thought, and the cadences of the familiar airs joined themselves together, and in the threefold communion we got that supreme achievement in lyrical art, the songs of Robert Burns. Burns is the folk-singer turned artist.

And because of that, because he is the singer of the songs of common folk, his appeal is of the kind that is for ever contemporaneous, not dependent for its vitality upon its association with any passing or past phase of history or with any particular school of culture; not dependent either upon the fact that it reflects the habits and customs of a given period, but upon the fact that it reflects the emotional instincts of the common people at *all* periods. It is of course of the highest value, from the point of view of Scottish nationality, that the national characteristics and ways of life should have found poetic expression just at the time when, in obedience to the pressure of industrial development, they were about to undergo some measure of—at least external—change, and it is of great importance for the preservation of Scottish nationality that the very spirit of the nation, its love of independence and liberty, should have been enshrined in never-dying song. It is these services that establish him in the mind of the whole world as the national poet of Scotland. But along with these there goes that expression of those natural impulses which are not determined by national or local environment, which are common to humanity everywhere, and have their source in the universal human heart. Artificialities, and fashions, and laws, these may come and go and come again; but the way of a man with a maid, the way of a mother with her child, the way of a friend with his friend, the companionship of man with man, the companionship of man with nature, these remain. The love-makings among the Ayrshire "Rigs o' Barley," or on the "Banks and Braes o' Bonnie Doon," have their counterparts the wide world over; and in every land, John Anderson and his jo spend canty days wi' ane anither, and go hand in hand down the hill of life. It is the rendering in song of all these commonplace—and because commonplace, therefore sacred—human experiences which constitutes Burns by universal consent, the poet of humanity.

The poet of humanity, and something more. For he was among the first to bring the lower animals into the fellowship. His sense of brotherhood was as wide as that. It was not restricted to the human species. In these days the endowment with human attributes of what we are pleased to call the brute creation has become quite a familiar phase in literature, and has been carried by Maeterlinck and Rostand into the region of the symbolical. It was Robert Burns who led the way. It is conceivable, for example, that "Rab and his Friends" would never have found a place in literature had they not been preceded by "Luath" and "Caesar" and *their* friends. If the birds of the air and the beasts of the fields could find articulate voice, or if we could imagine them as capable of handing on bird and beast traditions from generation to generation, surely the most grateful of their memories would have root in the time when the ploughman poet walked the Ayrshire fields. For ever since that time there has been a growing tenderness on the part of human beings towards the more helpless constituents in the scheme of nature. In Burns the predatory and primitive instincts of Man the Hunter disappear, and are replaced by the cultivated kindliness of Man the Brother—

> Avaunt, away! the cruel sway,
> Tyrannic man's dominion;
> The sportsman's joy, the murd'ring cry,
> The flutt'ring, gory pinion!

Here again we have Burns in the character of folk-singer. It is in the comradeship of common folk that the auld farmer's mare, and the ploughman's collie, and the "pet yowe," and even the field-mouse, enter into the songs of Burns. And not only the domesticated associates of the hearth and the stable and the farm-steading, but the wild, free "commoners of air," and the very troutlings in the running streams, are sharers in the kinship—

> On ilka hand the burnies trot,
> And meet below my theekit cot;
> The scented birk and hawthorn white
> Across the pool their arms unite,
> *Alike to screen the birdie's nest*
> *And little fishes' caller rest;*
> The sun blinks kindly in the biel',
> Where blythe I turn my spinnin'-wheel.

On lofty aiks the cushats wail,
And echo cons the doolfu' tale;
The lintwhites in the hazel braes,
Delighted, rival ither's lays;
The craik amang the claver hay,
The paitrick whirrin' o'er the ley,
The swallow jinkin' round my shiel,
Amuse me at my spinnin'-wheel.

This is a true folk-song; one of many in which the peasant-world and the world of nature intermingle and unify. Non-sentient nature also comes into the brotherhood: the woods and streams, and moors and mosses, and perfume-laden winds, they too are fraternal, not less than the "ourie cattle," the "jinkin' hares," the "deep-toned plovers," and "happin' wee things." With Burns, nature is not a world apart and outside of man—

O Nature! a' thy shews an' forms
To feeling, pensive hearts hae charms!
Whether the summer kindly warms,
Wi' life an' light,
Or winter howls wi' gusty storms,
The lang, dark night.

With Burns, nature is friendly, companionable, intimate, familiar; relating itself continually to the moods and passions and experiences of common folk, either in association or in contrast—

How can ye chant, ye little birds,
And I sae weary, fu' o' care?

And hereat, I think, we get to the very essence of Burns' genius. He relates himself to the common people, just as nature does. His genius is nature song-embodied; nature, as the common people know it. He responds and corresponds to their intuitions, impulses, and feelings. His power and strength and music; his humour and mirth and tenderness; his occasional grossness; his directness and simplicity, are reflections of the same qualities in the common people.

In them these qualities are diffused, distributed here and there. In him they are fused harmonised, and intensified. He is a Representative Man, alike in his nationalism and in his humanism. He is representative at once of the spirit of the Scottish nation and of the spirit of common humanity This may not be testing him by "highest standards," but it is testing him by standards that are permanent.

The power and influence of Robert Burns cannot die until the idea of nationality has died out of the minds of the Scottish people, nor until the idea of Brotherhood has lost its hold upon the human race. And as both these ideas are imperishable, so also is the power of Robert Burns.

"The poet," says Emerson, "is the eternal man." I should say that the genius of Burns typifies the eternal common man, he himself being, just because of that, one of the most uncommon of men, radiating in streams of poetic light all those varied emotional qualities which he has derived through his intuitive sympathy with ordinary human nature. With him the commonplace becomes poetic, and therefore no longer commonplace. Burns, not less than the transcendentalists, is a seer of visions—terrestrial, if you will, not celestial—visions of the possibilities of man as a social being. His conception of the poet's mission, as he himself describes it, is to preserve, with soul erect, "the dignity of man." I do not know that Art has ever yet set itself any more ennobling vision or truer purpose than that.

That he was a great artist as well as a great poet—that is to say, great in execution as well as in conception—needs not now to be argued. But the source of his artistic instinct has been for the most part overlooked. He was an artist just as every conscientious workman is potentially an artist. Not the least of the evils arising out of modern industrialism is the tendency to make all production a question of mechanics rather than of craftsmanship, and the workman himself a machine rather than a craftsman. Burns took pride in the artistry of his songs, just as, we may be sure, he took pride in ploughing his furrows straight; and the quality and quantity of the workmanship, either of songs or furrows, was never conditioned by the nature of the reward. It is impossible to think of Burns as measuring the value of his poetic output by so many shillings or guineas per stanza, as some modern poets are said to do. He never wrote a line for money, or for the prospect of money. He got some little money out of the published editions of his works, and was glad to get it, but it was not for that he wrote. Publishing was an afterthought. Literature as a profession, as a means of living, was no part of his personal scheme of life. He was willing always to earn his living in other ways, that he might keep his muse unsubservient to the despotism of natural necessity. He held to this ideal to the very last, and when he had settled down to the work of reclaiming and purifying the ancient folk-songs of Scotland, resented the bare suggestion of money payment. "Foolish and quixotic!" we say. But while we say it, we are proud and glad that Burns acted so; that here was one man whose devotion to Art was pure and disinterested. "The labourer is worthy of his hire." Yes; but here is where Burns stands out. He was a labourer in Poesy's vineyard; but a hireling never. His genius was not for sale. He gave it freely to his country and to humanity. There probably never was any true artist who did not, in his soul, wish that he could go and do likewise. For the high service which this Scottish peasant rendered to Art and to Humanity his memory deserves to be held in honour, whether by sculptured monuments or by annual 25th of January sacraments. But most of all by striving to give reality to his ideals. To drink to his memory is nothing, to write orations about him is nothing, to write books about him is nothing, unless along with these we in our own day and generation, with what talents and opportunities we are possessed, and with the help of his inspiration and that of other teachers, and in co-operation with all who are like-minded, seek for the ways and means to abolish poverty and establish Liberty and Brotherhood, not for some men, but for all mankind.

A poet's dream! If you say so, then it is a dream—*for you.* It is because we have held it for a dream that it remains unrealised. If it be a dream, then Robert Burns and all the world's poets have lived in vain.

To doubt that Liberty and Brotherhood are attainable is the most damnable heresy. It is high treason to the race, and amongst the multitude of modern infidelities is the only infidelity that matters.

> For a' that, and a' that,
> It's comin' yet for a' that,
> When man to man, the world o'er,
> Shall brithers be for a' that!

BOOK TWO

Fighters for Freedom

in Scotland

The Days of Baird and Hardie

INTRODUCTORY

This booklet was first published in 1908 by the Independent Labour Party. The centenary (1920) of the execution of Baird and Hardie, two of the men whom it commemorates, seems a fitting occasion for its being reprinted. The period with which it deals was not unlike the period through which we are now passing. It was a revolutionary period, and the aspirations of the workers in all lands drew much of their incentive from the upheavals in France and America, just as at the present time they are affected by events in Russia. The ruling classes of this country were also greatly influenced by the dynastic and political overthrow which had taken place in those other countries, and were correspondingly ruthless in their efforts to prevent the revolutionary movement from taking root in Great Britain. Neither the rulers nor the workers quite understood the nature of the changes which were taking place in the industrial fields, but instinctively the rulers felt that they must prevent the lower orders from obtaining any share in political or social administration. Thus then developed the great struggle between privilege and democracy, which has continued ever since, and must continue until democracy has won the victory. That the part played by some of the common men associated with that struggle may not be entirely forgotten is the chief reason for the writing of this book.

If thereby even one of my readers is stimulated to play a man's part in the present-day struggle for Liberty, which can only be fully realised in Socialism, I am satisfied.

Muir of Huntershill

On September 29th 1798, in the village of Chantilly, near Paris, there died Thomas Muir, of Huntershill, Glasgow.

I am not aware that there is any memorial of Thomas Muir in the city of his birth. Perhaps that is waiting for an age which will be better able to judge of the qualities which constitute a great man.

Even amongst those who ought to treasure his memory, Thomas Muir is not well known, nor the manner of his life and death. That is why I am writing this article. I have met many Socialists to whom the name of this man is little more than a vague tradition, and others I have met who have never even heard of him.

Yet it is little more than one hundred years since he died, and at that time, and for years after, the fame and the fate of him were common talk wherever there were men who believed in Liberty. To the Revolutionary patriots of France and America, Thomas Muir was well known, and I doubt not that a search amongst the archives both of the French Directory and the American Senate, then newly established, would reveal many references to the "brave young Scottish advocate," as Lafayette loved to call him.

Thomas Muir was a rising member of the Scottish Bar at a time when the Scottish Bar was the chief avenue to fame and place and power for able and ambitious men; the time which gave us Henry Erskine and Francis Jeffrey and Cockburn. Thomas Muir was quite as able as any of these men, but he was—different. They gained renown and reputation by their brilliant defence of political prisoners and felons.

Thomas Muir himself became a political prisoner and felon, and it is a fact that the same ship which carried him to Botany Bay carried also one of the convicts whom his eloquence as counsel had saved from the gallows for the crime of murder.

I think we ought to keep green the memory of such a man, not so much for his sake as for our own; to him it cannot matter. It is well, in these days, that we should not forget how short the time is since men could be sent to the scaffold and to Botany Bay for demanding constitutional government. For that was the sole crime of Thomas Muir, and of Skirving and Palmer and Gerald and Margarot, who shared his fate. Botany Bay was the Siberia of Great Britain, a place of exile for the criminal and the patriot.

Let us not be too proud of ourselves, we Scottish people, nor imagine, as we sometimes do, that Scotland has always been, or is even yet, the chosen land of liberty. We have not had our Grand Dukes, as in Russia, nor our Junkers, as in Germany, but we have had our Dundases, and at this time the family of Dundas were the bureaucracy of Scotland. It was they who exiled Muir and hanged Baird and Hardie and Wilson, and ruled the country with a rod of iron, themselves thriving on corruption, and this at the very time when Burns had set us singing "A man's a man for a' that."

Against all this knavery and tyranny Thomas Muir spoke out. He was able, eloquent, and earnest. He addressed great meetings throughout the country, always denouncing the corruption of the times, and demanding in the name of the people political reforms. In this work he stood practically alone, for even his personal friends the brilliant lights of the Scottish Bar, professed sympathisers with the cause of Reform, shrank from confronting the power of Henry Dundas, the Lord-Advocate, in whose hands lay the gifts of place and promotion.

The upshot of it all was that Muir was summoned to

appear before the Court of Justiciary on January 2nd, 1793, to answer the charge of sedition.

It was impossible for him to appear in Court on that date. He was then on a visit to Paris. We know now what great events were happening in Paris in 1792-3, and we can easily imagine the interests which took him there, and judge what manner of man was this who seemed to gravitate intuitively to the very heart and centre of the Revolutionary movement in that tumultuous time.

War had been declared between France and Britain. There were difficulties about passports, and it was the month of July, 1793, before he was able to land in Scotland to face his trial. By that time he had been declared an outlaw, and he had scarcely touched his native soil ere he was arrested, at Stranraer, and conveyed handcuffed and in irons to Edinburgh prison.

It was August 30th before he was brought to trial. Muir had to face a jury composed of men drawn from amongst the known and avowed enemies of reform, directed by a bench of judges similarly biased. Indeed, it was in the house of one of these same jurymen, Roehead of Innerleithen, that the Lord Justice Clerk discussed, over the toddy, whether the sentence on Margarot, one of Muir's associates, should include one hundred lashes; and it was this same dispenser of the law who declared that "the mob would be the better for some letting of blood." At the hands of such a tribunal the fate of Thomas Muir was as surely prejudged as was that of the Russian revolutionist at the hands of the Government of the Czar. The only thing in doubt was the measure and the method of severity to be dealt out to the prisoners. Muir himself knew this quite well, and though he spoke for three hours defending not himself, but the cause of Reform, all along the line, his closing words were a recognition that, so far as he was concerned, his pleading must be of no avail. "As for me," he said, "I am careless and indifferent to my fate. I can look danger and I can look death in the face, for I am shielded by the consciousness of my own rectitude. I may be condemned to languish in the recesses of a dungeon, I may be doomed to ascend the scaffold; nothing can deprive me of the recollection of the past—nothing can destroy my inward peace of mind, arising from the remembrance of having discharged my duty."

"Fourteen years' transportation beyond seas" was the sentence, one of the judges suggesting that the prisoner should be publicly whipped. Some of the best families in Edinburgh, we are told, were grieved and petrified by that sentence. But the "best families" in Edinburgh and elsewhere usually take care to keep their own skins whole. Their petrifaction must have been greater than their grief, for they did nothing to save Thomas Muir, and less than nothing to vindicate the liberties of the Scottish people—the weavers and common folk had to do that later with their lives. An effort was made in Parliament to have the verdict and sentence set aside; and it is worth remembering that only two Scottish Members voted in its favour. So much for the "best families." They have been like that always, and are still. The Scottish people owe no debt of gratitude to their nobility and gentry.

Thomas Muir was duly shipped from Newhaven to the hulks at London, and from thence, in company with other patriots, to Botany Bay. But that was not the end of Thomas Muir. Between the sailing of the convict ship and the last days at Chantilly there lie five years of amazing and marvellous adventure.

It is a most remarkable story, but the most I can do is to set down the main incidents briefly and baldly.

The facts themselves should be interesting enough. They are of the kind that need no literary embellishment.

It would be in the year 1794 that Muir and his companions were landed at Botany Bay. They were amongst the earliest of the Australian colonists, if we can call by that name men who were sent there as convicts. They found there a community of some 200 persons, all, with the exception of the Governor and his family, compulsory emigrants like themselves, though, of course, belonging to a different class, Muir and his friends being actually the first political prisoners sent out. There were many more to follow, right down to the Chartist times.

At first it almost seemed as if Muir was destined to settle down permanently in this new land. The Governor, who was a Scotchman from Leith, recognising that the newcomers were not exactly the kind of hardened criminals with whom he had usually to deal, left them very much to their own resources. They built cottages for themselves, and commenced to cultivate plots of land, and Muir found agreeable mental exercise in endeavouring to teach the more ignorant members of the settlement. For nearly two years this sort of life continued, and might have continued for many more. But one morning a ship flying the American flag cast anchor in the bay. Ostensibly in search of supplies of fresh water, its real mission was the rescue of Thomas Muir. It had been specially fitted out and commissioned for that purpose by the American Government, with the approval, if not the direct initiative, of George Washington. Muir was nothing loath. The others remained behind. Two of them, indeed, Gerald and Skirving, were at that moment sick unto death, and never rallied. So Muir alone made good his escape. To him the message from Washington must have seemed almost like a divine call. He was just thirty years of age, in the prime of manhood, and doubtless perfectly conscious of his powers and capabilities. The prospect of beginning life afresh in the brave new Republic of the West, among kindred spirits, must, apart from the natural desire for freedom, have appealed irresistibly to a man like Thomas Muir.

But these aspirations were not to be realised. The ship was wrecked in a storm on the western coast of America, near Nootka Sound, and of all on board only Muir and two sailors were cast up on the beach alive. After some days of wandering he somehow got separated from his two companions in misfortune, and he never saw them again. Nor were they ever heard of more. Their fate can only be guessed at. As for Muir, his perils and adventures were only beginning.

He shortly afterwards fell into the hands of a band of savages, probably the hunting party of some Indian tribe. The savages, so-called, did not harm Thomas Muir. They were good to him. They fed him and clothed him, and gave him of the best they had, and for weeks he moved about with them, and lived with them as one of themselves.

White men have before now, under similar circumstances, settled down to the primitive life of the woods and the prairie. But Muir was not that kind of white man. It was the America of civilisation he had come in search of, not the America of the backwoods.

So after a while he managed to give his redskin friends the slip, and set out on what was surely one of the most marvellous pilgrimages on record. For 2,000 miles, we are told, he travelled along the West Coast of America, foraging his food from wild nature, and with the sun and stars for his guides. Deep and strange thoughts must have filled the mind of this lonely man with the stormy past and the uncertain future, as he fought his way forward, he knew not where. He had one companion—the pocket Bible given him by his mother on Newhaven pier. He was a devout man, having been elder of

Cadder Parish Kirk at home, and there can be no doubt that for him, as he lay down at night under the stars the words of the Old Book would have very direct and special meaning. with its talk of pastures green and quiet waters, and its promise that the righteous man would never be forsaken, nay, not even in the Valley of the Shadow.

The end of his long wanderings brought him to Panama, the old Spanish-American city whose very name conjures up visions of Eldoradian romance. It was then still under the Spanish Government, and probably the fact that Britain and Spain were then at war inclined the Governor to listen sympathetically to the tale of Thomas Muir, whom he would naturally regard as a rebel, and therefore an enemy to Britain.

He had him sent across the Isthmus of Darien, under the escort of a party of Spanish soldiers, and landed at Vera Cruz, at that time the principal seaport of Mexico, in the hope that he would find there some American vessel bound for New York. There was no such vessel there, and he was sent on still further to the Havannah.

The Governor at this place, though treating Muir kindly and respectfully, seems to have regarded him somewhat as a prisoner, and decided that it was his duty to ship him to Spain, there to be dealt with by the Spanish Government. Muir was put on board one of two frigates bound for Cadiz, heavily laden with silver specie, and thus, after sampling the shores of two continents, our exiled Scottish reformer found himself once more with his face set towards Europe.

This is truly a strange and almost incredible tale. Those treasure-laden frigates never reached port. A British squadron, under the command of Sir John Jervis, lay in wait for them just outside Cadiz. A naval battle ensued, in which the Spaniards were defeated. Whether Muir was compelled to fight against his countrymen I know not. But he certainly fell amongst the fighting men, and in a letter sent home by a British officer he was reported to have been killed.

But Thomas Muir was not dead. Once again something like a miracle had happened to him. One of the British officers who boarded the vessel after the engagement proved to be an old Glasgow College companion of Muir's. He recognised his former fellow-student, not by his features, which were frightfully disfigured, but by the mother's inscription in his Bible, and finding there was still life in him, instead of taking him prisoner, he put him aboard a pinnace and sent him ashore to the Spanish authorities, with the urgent request that they would pay particular attention to him as one of their own wounded.

The news of Muir's extraordinary escape and woeful plight travelled speedily to France, which country was at that time, I think, in alliance with Spain against this country, and quietly there came the message from the French Directory, whose President was the great Napoleon, urging that all care should be taken of the Scottish patriot. Thus with the fate of Thomas Muir there is linked those two great names in history, George Washington and Napoleon Buonaparte. Following this message there came another, conferring upon Muir all the privileges of a free citizen of France. So after all he died a Republican.

There is little more to be told. He never recovered from his wounds, though he rallied sufficiently to enable him to set foot before he died in the land which had adopted him as its citizen. He travelled slowly to Paris, and was feted, caressed, and honoured on all hands, and by all classes, this man whom the laws of his native land had branded as a felon. At Chantilly he died, having given his life for human liberty. I think Thomas Muir was a great man. I am certain he was a brave and true man. He sacrificed everything for his cause. He was twenty-six years of age when he chose his side. He had gained front rank in his profession, and fortune's ball was at his feet. He knew well what it meant when he made his choice, and he never flinched nor faltered. If this imperfect tribute to his memory carry with it any gleam of inspiration even to one of those who may read, I am satisfied.

Two Glasgow Weavers

On the night of July 23rd, 1817—that is, one hundred and thirteen years ago, a man was trudging the high-road between Edinburgh and Glasgow, with his face set towards the west. He was a poor man: one of the poorest. He was tramping home to poverty, hardship, and hunger; yet he was probably the most joyful man in the three kingdoms that summer evening. For he had just escaped as by a miracle from the very jaws of death and he was going home to his wife and weans in the Calton of Glasgow. His name was Andrew M'Kinley, a Glasgow weaver, tried that day for his life on a charge of high treason, and now a free man. During the whole of five months he had lain a prisoner in Edinburgh Castle, the Calton jail not being considered strong enough to hold this desperate character. And now his enemies had been discomfited, and he was free! Yet his escape had been marvellous and unexpected, even by himself. Three years later, Baird, Hardie, and Wilson were to swing for the same offence with which he had been charged; others of his own class and craft and calling were to be sent to Botany Bay. Verily, he had reason to rejoice. Often and often I have tried to picture to myself those unhappy times. I have heard very old men talk about them, and I have read about them in books, but always there has come up before me, clear and vivid, the figure of that solitary wayfarer, pacing the long miles on the Glasgow road through the silent hours of that summer night.

The night mail-coach would go rattling past him, carrying before him to Glasgow the news of his acquittal; for these were not the days of express trains and telegraphs; and as he neared Shettleston the morning sun would uprise to greet him, and the wood birds sing to him a welcome song. So at least I love to fancy the dawn of that July morning, when the weary-footed Calton weaver, type of his class and his times, came home from jail.

How had he managed to escape? That is my story. Not assuredly by the clemency of his judges. They were men who knew not the meaning of the word. They were eager and anxious to convict, and so create the necessary precedent for stamping out by the death penalty the Reform movement in Scotland. Nor yet was it by the skill and eloquence of his counsel that Andrew M'Kinley was saved, though they were amongst the ablest of their time, and included Jeffrey, Cockburn, and Moncrieff, who, to their credit, had given their services free.

He was saved by the steadfastness and downright moral courage of another Glasgow weaver, John Campbell by name. He also had been detained a prisoner in Edinburgh Castle, on the same charge as M'Kinley; but he had been detained for the purpose of being used as the principal witness against his fellow-craftsman. None of the counsel for the defence had been allowed to have the slightest intercourse with him, and he was expected to swear that it was M'Kinley who had administered to him a so-called treasonable oath, pledging its subscribers to labour for "the elective franchise at the age of twenty-one, with free and equal representation to annual Parliaments." Both men had undoubtedly signed this most revolutionary document, which was afterwards proved to have been the concoction of a paid Government spy, a fact of which the prosecution were doubtless even then quite well aware. But at present the object was to obtain a conviction against M'Kinley as the ringleader in a great political conspiracy. Afterwards the net could have been spread widely enough.

John Campbell was to be the instrument to this end. He had been cajoled, and bullied, and bought, and he was quite safe to do as he was told. So thought the prosecution. But John Campbell was not that kind of man. He kept his own counsel, but he had quite made up his mind what to do, and he even contrived to convey to M'Kinley, in another part of the Castle, a small crumb of hope, in the shape of a scrap of paper, enclosed in a quid of tobacco, on which was written the following words: "They are wanting to bribe me to swear away your life, but I'm true." Brave John Campbell! Wise as the serpent, but not so harmless as the dove. He was playing craft against craft, and biding his time.

When the day of the trial came, John Campbell shattered all their schemes and contrivings by a single word. The defending counsel, with the best of intentions, did all they could to prevent this witness from being brought forward. He was the one witness to save their case and their client. "Have you," said the presiding judge, blandly, putting the usual preliminary questions to the witness—"have you any malice or ill-will to the prisoner at the bar?" "None, my lord," said John Campbell. "Has anybody given you any reward or promise of reward, for being a witness in this trial?" The moment had come. Quick, clear, decisive, and resolute came the answer, "Yes, my Lord."

In an instant the accusers had become the accused. The Glasgow weaver had taken his stand, and he was not to be bullied out of it by any bench of judges or prosecuting lawyers. Briefly, in reply to Jeffrey's questions, he told how, in the presence of the Sheriff of Edinburgh, he had been promised by the Advocate-Depute—who was present in Court—a good permanent Government situation abroad, through Lord Sidmouth, after he gave his evidence for the Crown that day on that trial. There was no more to be said. The Crown lawyers threw up the sponge. The case collapsed like a house of cards. John Campbell had kept his word. He was true. And Andrew M'Kinley walked out of court a free man.

A curious, queer, old story, isn't it? and worth re-telling, if only for the light it sheds on the political methods of the governing classes of those bad old times. They wouldn't do such things nowadays. Perhaps they don't need. They have filched away the material results of the reforms for which M'Kinley and his contemporaries fought, and they have left the worker with a vote—which he uses against himself. He is free, but not with the kind of freedom the old weavers dreamt of. Perhaps, if they had thought that this was to be all—this, that we have to-day—they wouldn't have risked their necks about it The modern capitalists would never think of bribing a workman to give false evidence against his fellows.

Why should they, when there is an easier and a safer way? They have only to induce him to vote Liberal or Tory. I confess I see little difference between 1817 and 1920, except that the new way is less clumsy, is cuter and more plausible than the old way. And the worker, if he strikes, can still be starved into submission. or, if need be, shot down. It was so in the time of Andrew M'Kinley and it is so still; and poverty and hardship and hunger are there; and slums such as he couldn't even have imagined on that morning when he came home to his wife and children.

Hunger is hunger whether it be endured by one or by a thousand, and there is not so much excuse for it now as there was then. We have votes, which the early reformers had not. We ought to have used our votes to abolish hunger. I am quite certain that was what the Glasgow weavers wanted to vote for—to abolish hunger. For my part, if the vote cannot do that, I don't see the use of it.

Well, I meant only to tell a story, not to moralise or sermonise. I have at least done what I have long had a mind to do: paid my tribute of respect to the memory of these brave Glasgow weavers. May we play our part as well as they did, and may each of us be able to say, as said sterling John Campbell, in the face of tyranny and wrong, "I am True!"

Wilson o' Strathaven

I dare say not many of my English readers have heard of Strathaven—or Str'aven, as the local dialect pronounces it. Strathaven is an old Lanarkshire village, or township, about twenty-four miles south-east of Glasgow. For hundreds of years the whirr of the hand-loom weaver's shuttle has been heard in Strathaven. It is still heard there, though nowadays its music sounds somewhat melancholy, as if intermingled with it were the dirge of a dying time. To me, Strathaven's chief interest lies in the fact that it was the home of James Wilson, who in the year 1820 suffered death in the Jail Square of Glasgow for the cause of Reform.

Poor James Wilson. For sixty years he lived in this village of Strathaven, in the same house all that time, under the one roof of thatch, weaving manfully his web of cloth and his web of life; and then they took and hanged the old man for a traitor. It was out of sheer cowardliness that they slew him. Tyranny, panic-stricken, afraid of it knew not what, had to find its victims, and it found them in Wilson, Baird, and Hardie, and of these three the most harmless was the old Strathaven weaver.

Never was there a man in whose nature there was less of the political desperado; the kind of quiet citizen who in ordinary times passes through life placidly and cheerfully, with few ups and downs, and dies in his bed, with his friends around him. Yet he died on the scaffold, with thousands looking on, and though they knew it was murder that was being perpetrated before their eyes, no intervening hand was raised to save him. Little wonder the ruling classes have looked upon the common people as if they were beasts of burden.

The story of Wilson is soon told. He was the victim

of that system of espionage to which in all countries and in all ages, terrified tyrannical governments have resorted in order to find the means to justify their tyranny in the eyes of the world. Wilson was, like all intelligent workmen of his time, a believer in Parliamentary Reform. In his younger days he had been in correspondence with Thomas Muir and Skirving and the other champions of the cause who, in 1793, were sent to Botany Bay for their fearless advocacy of the principles of political freedom. The movement, at that time driven under, was again raising its head. All over the land, in every weaver's loom shop, and around every shoemaker's bench, the talk was of Reform, just as with us to-day the talk is all of Socialism and Labour Representation, and workshop control, and in Strathaven Wilson's house was the rendezvous of the local reformers, a kind of I.L.P. club in the days before Socialism had been dreamed of.

In those circumstances, the agents provocateurs of the Government, of whom there are always plenty in times like those, organised a sham rebellion, and managed to give it so much the appearance of actuality that many of the genuine reformers were induced to take part. Amongst these were Baird of Condorrat, Hardie of Glasgow, and Wilson. The Strathaven man, indeed, joined almost under compulsion. The thought of violent action was foreign to the very nature of the man, and it was only the feeling of loyalty to the cause which led him and some score of his fellow villagers to march out one April morning to join the main body of the rebels, represented by the Government's spies to be encamped in strong force on Cathkin Braes. They had scarcely set out when their native common sense revealed to them either that they had been duped, or the foolhardiness of their enterprise, and they returned to their homes, Wilson being hardly allowed to recross his threshold before he was arrested in the name of the Government whose officials had laid the trap for him.

The old man had never a chance for his life. It is true that the jury, along with their verdict of guilty, recommended him to mercy. But a Government which is bent on intimidating public opinion knows nothing of mercy, and the Strathaven weaver had to die. And he died like a brave man, unflinchingly and with dignity. In his declaration he avowed himself to be no traitor; but he also avowed that the cause of Reform was a just cause. "I acknowledge," he said, with a certain simple pride, "that I die a patriot, for the cause of freedom for my poor country, and I hope that my countrymen will continue to see the necessity of a Reform in the way of the country being represented; and I hope my dear countrymen will unite and stand firm to their rights." Unite and stand firm to their rights! Well said, old man! That will do for a slogan to-day as well as for a hundred years ago; and though we may not be called upon, as you were, to die for the cause, we can nevertheless give our lives to it.

They buried him in the paupers' burying-ground, near to the cathedral of Glasgow. But he did not rest there long. A rebel he may have been, but he was no pauper. And that same night, when darkness had fallen, two brave and tender women—James Wilson's own daughter and his niece—did what surely women-folk never did before nor since: they with their own hands dug up the poor maltreated body of him whom they loved, and ere the morning sun had risen James Wilson was home again in Str'aven. And there he lies to this day. When you pass that way, uncover in reverence, not only to the memory of one of Freedom's martyrs, but also in remembrance of those gentle, resolute, leal-hearted Scottish women.

Twelve years later the Reform came. But it was not the Reform for which the Str'aven weaver died. That reform has not come even yet. Bitter disappointment was the lot of the reformers after '32, and the Chartists had to take up the work in the doing of which Baird and Hardie and Wilson fell. The Chartists, too, were martyred and defeated. Reform came, and still more Reform. And still Labour remains outside, the Lazarus not of parable but of fact, gathering the crumbs from the rich man's table.

Baird and Hardie

Visitors to Glasgow who desire to get an impression of the immensity of the city usually betake themselves to the Necropolis, that picturesque graveyard overlooking the cathedral, and commanding a view south and west of miles on miles of clustering house-tops and steeples and factory chimneys.

One hundred years ago the city was much smaller, and there was no graveyard up there, but only a secluded bit of woodland, well outside the city and known as Fir Park. It was here that in the dark of an April night in 1820 the rebels mustered to set out on their expedition for the freeing of their country from oppression. They were not more than fourscore in number, and they had been got together at the instigation of certain men of their own class—Richmond, Craig, Turner, King, and others. Years afterwards these men were proved to have been paid Government spies and agents provocateurs but the Glasgow weavers and artisans could not know that. On the contrary, they had every apparent reason for placing their faith in these men. They were of themselves; and one of them, Richmond, had himself stood his trial for "combination," and narrowly escaped transportation. There was nothing to show that they had been bought by the Government, or that they were other than what they professed to be—bona-fide representatives of the National Revolutionary Movement.

Nor were the rebel weavers the only people who were deceived. For some days previously the walls had been mysteriously placarded with an address to the people, calling upon them to "assert their rights at the hazard of their lives," and purporting to be issued "By Order of the Committee of Organisation for forming a Provisional Government." The authorities of the city issued a counter proclamation, appealing to the loyalty of the citizens, and prohibiting "parties or groups of people from standing together or walking on the streets after the hour of seven." The town was filled with military, and a special volunteer corps was organised for the defence of public and private property. Glasgow was in a state of siege.

In this state of matters, it was easy for the Glasgow weavers to believe in the existence of a great national rising, and they certainly knew that in the condition of the people there was cause for such a rising. But there was no organised revolutionary movement, only a sham revolutionary movement, engineered by the Government itself. "Ridiculous!" you say. "Impossible!" Not at all, my friends. These things happened under the infamous administration of Sidmouth and Castlereagh, those two men to whom the terrible symbolism of Shelley had given ghastly immortality—

> I met Murder on the way—
> He had a mask like Castlereagh.
> Very smooth he looked, yet grim;
> Seven bloodhounds followed him.
>
> * * * *
>
> Clothed with the Bible, as with light,
> And the shadows of the night,
> Like Sidmouth next, Hypocrisy,
> On a crocodile came by.

Under a regime which could call forth such bitterness as that, all evil deeds were possible. The Government of the nation was itself a system of underground conspiracy, and this manufactured revolt of the Glasgow weavers was one of its results.

As for the fourscore rebels assembled in Fir Park, they had no doubts about the matter. They had their definite instructions from the pretended Committee of Provisional Government. They were to make for Falkirk, there to meet the English revolutionaries, said to number many thousands, and to seize the cannon in Carron

Ironworks. On their way they were to march through Condorrat, where they would be joined by John Baird and other reformers. They had no means of knowing that the English revolutionary force at Falkirk was purely a fiction; still less could they know that, supposing they ever reached Carron, a troop of Hussars was posted inside the works ready to receive them; or that the military authorities at Stirling had their plans laid for waylaying them on the march. Through all the hateful business the simple heroism of the Glasgow weavers stands out clear and true. They believed that the hour had come, and they left father and mother and wife and child and forsook all to follow the cause.

Andrew Hardie had said good-bye to his old mother and to his sweetheart, his "dear and loving Margaret," and John Baird had taken farewell of his brother and sister and other companions. These two men met for the first time on that April morning at Condorrat. They became on the instant sworn friends, and were appointed leaders by their comrades, and it was this spontaneous leadership which marked them out for extreme punishment by the vindictive Government authorities.

In the early dawn they halted for some refreshments at Castlecary, but by this time the Government agents had slipped away on pretence of being required for further organising work in Glasgow. The original company had dwindled down to about half its numbers, which was not surprising, for there was no sign of any general rising, the furnaces of Carron were blazing as usual, and the great concourse of rebels which they expected to find was nowhere visible. Given another hour, the remnant of travel-worn men might have realised that they had been fooled, and would have quietly disbanded. But this would not have suited the purpose of those who had laid the trap for them. At the hill of Bonnymuir they were met by a troop of horse from Stirling Castle, and, in the excitement of the moment, with no time for deliberation, they determined to fight and fall rather than to surrender without a fight. And fight they did, that handful of weary, ill-armed, and inexperienced men, against the well-equipped, well-mounted, and disciplined soldiery. They fought so hard that almost every man of them was wounded, some very severely, before they surrendered. The commanding officer of Hussars was also wounded, and his horse shot under him.

The end was inevitable. They were surrounded and captured, and nightfall found them lodged in Stirling Castle, as prisoners of war, to be shortly transferred to Edinburgh, preparatory to their being tried as traitors.

This was the battle of Bonnymuir deemed to be of so much importance as a great victory for law and order that the bells were set ringing in all the steeples, and a special issue of the "Gazette" was published to assure the nations of Europe that the treasonable Provisional Government in Scotland had been destroyed.

There never was any Provisional Government. Whether there might have been some day a body of the kind can only now be a matter of conjecture. The Provisional Government was a fictitious creation of the real Government, and it served their purpose. It served to induce a body of working men to take up arms in open rebellion, and thereby gave the authorities apparent justification for proceeding to the most extreme measures of repression. Up till now they had not been able to hang a reformer. Their chance had now come.

It also served to terrify the middle classes, to set them more bitterly against the workers than before, and to modify their conception of Reform. It was due to the feeling of fear thus engendered that the Reform Bill of twelve years later, for which more working-class blood had to be shed, was so conceived and framed that the workers were left completely outside, and had to begin over again the work for which Muir, and Margarot, and Baird, and Hardie, and Wilson had suffered—the work which has not even yet been accomplished, so easily bamboozled and duped is the British democracy.

The trial of Baird and Hardie and their comrades took place on July 6th, just three months after their capture at Bonnymuir. In the interval they had undergone examination at Edinburgh by the Crown officials, and also at Stirling by a special Royal Commission, which, being composed of avowed enemies of Reform, had as a matter of course found true bills for high treason against all the prisoners. This same precious Commission, previous to the trial, issued an injunction to the Press, interdicting and prohibiting the publication of any of the evidence, or any of the speeches of counsel, till the whole of the trials were over.

In such fashion was carried through the administration of justice (so-called) in the days of our grandfathers, and it was in the face of this spirit of overbearing intolerance that these eighteen working men had to stand up for their lives—before men who had already prejudged them.

From the outset it was made evident that what was wanted was a conviction. Somebody had to be hanged, and, in addition to the Scottish officers of the Crown, an English barrister of note, Mr. Sergeant Hullock, was brought down to see that no possible legal loophole was left through which the prisoners might escape. Francis Jeffrey, to his credit, without fee or reward, led for the defence, and, of course, did his best in a case that was hopeless from the beginning. Hardie came first, it being agreed that the verdict in his case should govern all the others, an arrangement which in itself was an injustice, for there were points against him in which the others were not involved.

For example, on the Sunday previous to the Bonnymuir business he had in Cathedral Street interfered to prevent the pulling down of the alleged treasonable poster until he should have read it, and this was held to be proof of his participation in its production. Baird never even saw the poster, yet his conviction was to be determined by the conviction of Hardie. Methods such as this characterised the whole proceedings. Says a contemporary writer: "Undoubtedly there was much hard swearing in the case against them: every legal point was dexterously driven home against them by Sergeant Hullock." But, indeed, there could be no real defence. They were taken with arms in their hands; their own wounds were evidence against them. The most that Jeffrey could do was to plead eloquently for leniency, to argue skilfully that their offence did not amount to treason, to do what eloquence and persuasive advocacy might do to bring his clients clear of the death sentence. It was said that he spoke most ably. He might as well have spoken to stone walls, and he knew it, and told his clients from the beginning to be prepared for the worst.

Upon all the eighteen prisoners sentence of death was pronounced, to be afterwards commuted to transportation for life in the case of all except Baird and Hardie. For them a special aggravation even of the death sentence was enjoined. They were to be hanged and beheaded both, "and your bodies shall be divided into four parts, to be disposed of as His Majesty may think fit." To intimidate the workers: that was the purpose in view. It was against the people, the common rabble, that this vindictive savagery was directed. It was to be what we call an object lesson. The two poor weavers simply happened to be the victims—the illustrations, so to speak, of the ruthlessness and power of the law.

There were not wanting those even amongst the wealthy classes who recognised that the law was being degraded into an instrument of vengeance, and could no longer be regarded as a medium for administering justice. Strenuous efforts were made to obtain a reprieve for Baird and Hardie; one gentleman, Mr. Robert Grahame of Whitehill, even making a journey to London to plead with some of his friends in the Cabinet for clemency. What these too tender-hearted gentlefolks failed to realise was that this was not meant as an act of justice; it was an act of war—war against the people. There could be no reprieve for Baird and Hardie.

The only men who bore themselves throughout the whole of this tragedy with real natural dignity were the condemned men themselves. There is not on record, so far as I know, a single word of complaint from any one of them. They had taken this risk for the cause, and they accepted as men should the fate that had come to them. Their letters written from prison reveal them as men much more solicitous for the future welfare of their friends left behind than for any vindication of their own conduct. That, they believed, might well be left to the judgment of history.

Occasionally in some of their letters there leaps out a phrase which preserves as in a picture the daily environment in which these rebel weavers had spent their lives. "Be sure," says Hardie, in one of his letters—"be sure to be kind to my poor canary." Kindly Andra Hardie! 'Tis a hundred years since, yet even at this moment I seem to hear the blithe song o' the bird, in the old loom-shop in the High Street, striving to outrival the whirr and clatter of the shuttle and treadles. And, again, these last words to the girl he was to have married: "Farewell—a long farewell to you and all worldly cares, for I have done with them. I hope you will call frequently on my poor distressed and afflicted mother. At the expense of some tears I destroyed your letters. Again farewell, my dearest Margaret. May God attend you still, and all your soul with consolation fill, is the sincere prayer of your most affectionate and constant lover while on earth.—Andrew Hardie."

There is a whole world of past joys and coming sorrows for these two working-class women wrapped up in these simple phrases; the joys and sorrows that come to nearly all women of their class, even though the sons and lovers be not martyrs and felons.

Twelve years later, during the rejoicings over the Reform Bill, the old mother had in her window:—

> Britons, rejoice, Reform is won!
> But 'twas the cause
> Lost me my son.

Alas! old mother, the reform that came was not worth the life of so brave a man.

Yet through all these closing letters, with death in front of them, there was never any word of regret for the part they had played, never the slightest surrender of principles. Permit me one more quotation. I want to make it plain to the reader what kind of men they were. They belonged to my class, and I would rather commemorate their memory than that of all the great men of any other class. In a postscript to a letter of Baird's to his friend Taylor, of Kilsyth, Hardie adds: "Dear Sir,—This comes from a hand you never saw . . . Hard is our fate, my dear unknown friend, yet I resign my life without the least reluctance . . . I hope you will keep in your remembrance the cause for which Baird and Hardie and Clelland died on the scaffold." (Clelland, the smith, was respited almost at the last moment.) To the last they never flinched from this attitude. It was the cause, always the cause.

To most people the names of these two Scottish weavers have a certain dim heroic significance; but as to the nature of their heroism, and the character of the social and political environment wherein that heroism was enacted, few have more than the vaguest appreciation.

There were many others, as good and brave men as Baird and Hardie, who died for the good cause, whose names are—and must for ever remain—unknown; men shot down in the streets amidst tumult and riot, or obscurely lingering out their days in poverty and pain.

Baird and Hardie's names live on because of the publicly tragic manner of their death under the gaze of the whole nation. There must be something in the circumstances leading up to that tragedy which we ought to know, and ought never to forget.

Suppose we begin by asking why in our minds these two names are inseparable? It is not possible to speak or write of them separately. We cannot think of the one apart from the other. Yet they were not life-long friends. Up to within five months of the moment when they shook hands for the last time on the scaffold at Stirling, they had never met, nor even heard of each other. They had not been associated as leaders in the Reform movement; indeed, neither of them was ever a leader, except involuntarily for a few brief hours, and it was those few brief hours that sealed their fate. Hardie was a weaver in Glasgow; Baird was a weaver in Condorrat, a village a few miles further east. Baird was 32 years of age, Hardie was 28, and up to the month of April of the same year of their death, 1820, neither of them had done any more than is being done to-day by thousands of Socialist workmen. They had simply taken an intelligent part in the political and social life of their own immediate districts. Why was it then that these two men, who had lived all their lives apart, were brought together to suffer death in a cause in which they had taken only a subordinate part? How was it, too, that throughout the whole of that long period of unrest bordering on revolution, only three men were publicly executed, and these three men were working men—Baird, Hardie, and Wilson. The question itself suggests the answer. It was the working-class element in the Reform movement of which the governing classes were most afraid. It was the working classes who were to be intimidated. Remember this.

Baird and Hardie were not the only men condemned for high treason at Stirling. There were the other sixteen, and they were all working men. Of the eighteen men, there were nine weavers, one stocking weaver, one cabinet-maker, one labourer, two smiths, one muslin singer, one shoemaker, one tailor, one bookbinder—handicraftsmen all, except Benjamin Moir, the labourer. There were plenty of other men belonging to the higher ranks of society, brilliant barristers and literary men, talking and writing eloquent treason every day, yet none of them ever reached the scaffold. Do not mistake me. I do not forget that other Hardy, of London, and later, Ernest Jones, and other middle-class men who went to prison. What I do say is that the Government recognised that it was from the workers these leaders derived their strength, and when it came to striking their hardest, they struck at the workers.

Eight years before the hanging of the weavers at Stirling, they had shot and sabred the weavers in the Calton streets of Glasgow, and in many another town throughout the country. The Government feared the Reform movement, but they feared the working-class element in that movement more, for the working-class element meant not reform but revolution. It could not be otherwise. They were then in the midst of the industrial revolution, and political power in the hands of the workers meant the carrying of that revolution speedily to its logical end. Robert Owen was at New Lanark bravely trying to find a way out. But the governing classes did not want to find a way out. The workers were in the deepest distress. It was for bread for life itself, they were fighting. The Government were in mortal terror. They believed—and rightly, I think—that political reform that would include the workers could end in only one way. To them, as to the workers, Reform really meant Revolution; therefore, they quite logically stood out against reform until it could be made quite certain that the working classes could be excluded. At this particular juncture what the Government did was to start a bogus revolution of their own, and it was in the meshes of this bogus revolution that Baird and Hardie and Wilson were caught, and those eighteen working men found themselves indicted for high treason at Stirling.

On September 8th, 1820, Baird and Hardie were executed in the spacious square of Broad Street, just under the walls of Stirling Castle, and in the presence of a great assemblage of people. Both men spoke to the multitude.

Said Baird: "What I have hitherto done, and which has brought me here, was for the cause of truth and justice. I declare I never gave my assent to anything inconsistent with truth and justice." Said Hardie: "My dear friends, I declare before my God I believe I die a martyr in the cause of truth and justice." His voice must have sounded clear and strong across the whole square, for a great answering shout came back from the people, and the dragoons drew their swords, and the sheriff interfered to prevent Hardie from saying more in this strain. "My friends," said Hardie once more, "I hope none of you are hurt by this exhibition. Please, after it is over, go quietly home, and read your Bibles, and remember the fate of Hardie and Baird."

They kissed each other and shook hands, these two men, and then they died together for their beloved cause—for your cause and mine, comrades of to-day; for the cause of human liberty.

The Present Time

These events happened one hundred years ago.

What about the state of matters at the present time? When the workers in Glasgow, demanding a forty-hours' working week, demonstrated in a peaceful and constitutional way, they were met by the batons of the police, and the city was placed under military control.

When the miners of Great Britain threatened to come on strike for increased wages, shorter hours, and the nationalisation of the mines, they were told that the armed forces of the nation would be used against them, and, as is well known, preparations were made to carry the threat into execution. Whenever there is any serious dispute between the employers and any section of the workers, what are called the "forces of the Crown" are placed at the disposal of the employers. It has been so during all these intervening hundred years at every stage of the struggle between privilege and democracy. It is so to-day. Many things have changed during one hundred years, but the spirit of the propertied class has not changed. It is still intolerant, masterful, and unscrupulous. It still relies upon physical force for its maintenance. The elements which constitute the propertied class have somewhat changed. It is no longer only a landed class or a territorial class. It is a capitalist class. During these hundred years the capitalist system has fully developed itself. In the course of the development great vested interests have grown up, controlling land, and minerals, and railways, and transport. Landed interests, coal and iron and steel interests, railway interests, shipping interests, brewery interests, oil interests, financial interests, each organised for monopolist purposes, and finally, all combined for mutual defence, and for mutual predatory offensive against the natural rights of the common people. These vested interests thus combined constitute the propertied class of to-day. The capitalist class, restrained only in its power to enslave humanity by the growth of another power—the power of organised labour.

During these hundred years the workers have slowly and steadily organised themselves. Being more numerous than the propertied class, and more and more sectionally disposed, it has been difficult for them to fuse into one common force, but that has now nearly been achieved. The small trade unions have become big trade unions. The big unions in each separate industry have become federated or amalgamated. And these again have been united in Trades Unions, Congresses, and Labour Parties, their purpose being to secure at once control of industry and control of government. Unity of Labour for that purpose on the industrial and on the political field gives us the Socialist movement. The achievement of that purpose will give us Socialism. Thus we have these two great forces —Capitalism and Organised Labour—opposing each other. It is the same conflict in which a hundred years ago the Glasgow weavers gave their lives. We do well to remember them, and to honour them, and to draw inspiration from their example.

INSCRIPTIONS ON THE BAIRD AND HARDIE MONUMENT IN SIGHTHILL CEMETERY, GLASGOW.

The front inscription, No. 1:—

Erected by Public Subscription,
July, 1847,
To the Memory of
JOHN BAIRD, Aged 32,
and
ANDREW HARDIE, Aged 28,
Who, for the Cause of Freedom, suffered Death at
Stirling, 8th September, 1820.

The right-hand inscription, No 2:—

This Monument was repaired at considerable expense in 1865 by a few Friends under the superintendence of the original Hardie and Baird and Martyrs Stone Committees, and again in 1885 by subscriptions.

Inscription, No. 3:—

During the erection of this Monument the Committee applied to her Majesty's Government for permission to remove the mortal remains of the two Martyrs from Stirling to this spot, and, after a lengthened correspondence, the following letter was received from the Lord Advocate:—

Gwyder House, Whitehall,
London, 5th May, 1847.

Sir,—I have laid the Memorial from the relatives of ANDREW HARDIE and JOHN BAIRD before Secretary, Sir George Gray, and I have the satisfaction of informing you that if the Kirk Session of Stirling see no objections upon other grounds opposition will not be made on the part of the Government to the removal of the remains of these unfortunate men from their present place of interment, but the permission is given under the express condition that the removal shall take place without any public notice or intimation, and without any procession, or concourse, or attendance of people, but in the presence of a few friends only.

ANDREW RUTHERFORD.

In accordance with these instructions, the exhumation took place at an early hour on the morning of the 20th July, 1847, and the remains re-interred in front of this Monument on the same day in presence of a considerable assembly of friends.

Here then they rest! and far in future years
Shall Freedom dew this spot with memory's tears!

4th Inscription, left hand:—

Here lie the slain and mutilated forms
Of those who fell, and fell like martyrs true,
Faithful to freedom through a time of storms,
They met their fate as patriots always do.

Calmly they view'd Death's dread and dank array,
Serene in hope, they triumphed o'er dismay;
Their country's wrongs alone drew forth their sighs
And those to them endeared by Nature's holiest ties.

But truth and right have better times brought round,
Now no more traitors scorned by passing breath,
For weeping Scotland hails this spot of ground
And shrines, with all who fell for Freedom's faith,
Those sons of her's now fam'd made glorious by their death.

COPY OF CONTEMPORARY BROADSHEET

Trials and Sentences.

A full and particular account of the Trials and sentences of the Radicals at Stirling, who received sentence yesterday; twenty two of whom are to be hanged, beheaded, and quartered on the 8th September, 1820.

STIRLING, JULY 13.

The Lords Commissioners appointed by the Special Commission of Oyer and Terminer, for trying all Treasons and Misprisons of Treason, committed within the counties of Stirling, Lanark, Dumbarton, Renfrew, and Ayr, opened their proceedings here on Thursday morning. The following were the Lords Commissioners—The Lord President, Lord Justice Clerk, Lord Chief Baron, Lord Chief Commissioner of the Jury Court, Lord Hermand, Lord Gillies, Lord Pitmilly, Lord Succoth, and Lord Meadowbank. John Hullock, Esq., Serjeant at Law, assisted at the trials, and Mr. Thomas George Knapp, Clerk to the Arraigns of the Home Circuit in England, acted as Clerk to the Arraigns.

The Court was opened about nine o'clock, and in a few minutes was crowded with people. The Lord President then addressed the Court, laying down the law of High Treason. The evidence went to connect the Bonnymuir business with the proposed Radical insurrection in the West of Scotland, Hardie having violently resisted a Magistrate in Glasgow, who wished to take down one of the posted Radical proclamations of the 1st of April. The evidence afterwards traced him, and about 24 armed men, on their march from Castlecarry, where they got refreshment, and took a formal receipt for the reckoning, and from thence to Bonnymuir.

Mr. Jeffrey, for the panel, addressed the Court at great length, he admitted that the prisoner was found in arms in a skirmish with the King's troops at Bonnymuir, but denied that this constituted the crime of High Treason. The Solicitor General replied.

At one o'clock on Friday, the Jury retired for 10 minutes, when they returned their verdict, finding him guilty on the 1st count, for levying after which the following prisoners were called to the bar:—

John Baird, weaver in Condorrat.
Thomas M'Culloch, stocking-weaver in Glasgow.
Andrew Hardie, weaver there.
John Barr, weaver in Condorrat.
William Smith, weaver there.
Benjamin Moir, labourer in Glasgow.
Allan Murchy, blacksmith there.
Alex. Latimer or Lettimer, weaver there.
Alexander Johnston, weaver there.
Andrew White, Bookbinder there.
David Thomson, weaver there.
James Wright, tailor there.
William Clackson or Clarkson, shoemaker there.
Thomas Pike or Pink, muslin-singer there.
Robert Gray, weaver there.
James Clelland, smith there.
Alexander Hart, cabinet-maker there.
Thomas M'Farlane, weaver at Condorrat.

The indictment having been read over (charging them with treason in four different counts) the prisoners severally pleaded Not Guilty. Hardie's trial was first proceeded in.

Mr. Jeffrey, in a long speech, insisted that Mr. Serjeant Hullock was not entitled to plead before the Court, he being an English Barrister. The objection was repelled.

The Lord Advocate then addressed the Jury, war; and also on the 4th, for compassing to levy war against the King, in order to compel him to change his measures.

FRIDAY, AUGUST 4.

This day the Court met, and on the above-named persons being placed at the bar, the Lord President, after a most solemn address, said, "the sentence of the law is—That you be drawn on a Hurdle to the place of execution, on the 8th September, and after being hanged by the neck till dead, that your heads be severed from your bodies, and your bodies to be cut in quarters, to be at the disposal of the King; and the Lord have mercy on your souls." The prisoners were then taken from the bar, without showing any signs of agitation. They were all recommended to mercy, except Baird and Hardie.

William Crawford, weaver in Balfron.
John Anderson, weaver in St. Ninian's.
John M'Millan, nailer in Camelon.
James Burt, nailer there.
John Johnston, shoemaker in Falkirk.
James Aitken, grocer or merchant there.
James Aitken, wright in Camelon, and
Andrew Dawson, nailer there.

Were then put to the bar, charged with being concerned in the late Radical Rebellion, when four persons, viz.—William Crawford, John Anderson, John M'Millan and Andrew Dawson, received the same sentence as the above, but were strongly recommended to mercy.

GLASGOW, PRINTED BY JOHN MUIR.

BOOK THREE

The Nativity of Adam

The Nativity of Adam

"No one," says Charles Lamb, "ever regarded the First of January with indifference. It is that from which all date their time and count upon what is left. It is the nativity of our common Adam." With us in the north it is not possible, even if we would, to regard the First of January with indifference. We have made it a national affair. It is to us what Christmas is to the Southerner. It is our winter festival, and might probably be adduced by our critics to prove that we are at bottom mere Pagans, and cursed with more than our share of that original sin which it is said was "our common Adam's" fateful bequest to the human family. A Saxon friend of mine has quite a different though not more flattering theory. He maintains that New Year's Day in Scotland is really a religious festival.

The Scots, he declares, have personified New Year's Day as a kind of Father Confessor to whom they make confession of all the misdemeanours and shortcomings of the past year. It is the day for the remission of sins. The annual slate-cleaning day upon which, after acknowledging ourselves to be miserable sinners, and after making penitential vows of good conduct for the coming year, we straightway proceed with clear consciences, and a lofty sense of rectitude, to break all our good resolutions and run up a fresh record of transgressions in readiness for next New Year's Day.

I think my friend's theory is all wrong. To suppose that Scotsmen ever commit sins, or that if they do commit them they ever confess them, even to themselves, shows a lamentable ignorance of the national character.

No; we celebrate New Year's Day simply because it is New Year's Day. That is the beginning and the end of it. No other justification is needed. It is the first day of the year, and we want to be merry on that one day whatever may betide on all the others.

As to our methods of being merry, that is a different question. Truth to tell, I think there is ground for the accusation made against us, in common with Englishmen, that we take our pleasures sadly. Last New Year's Eve—Hogmanay as we call it—I made one of a vast crowd that had assembled in the vicinity of Glasgow Cross to welcome in the New Year. For hours previously this crowd had been slowly gathering by the five main thoroughfares that converge upon the Tron Kirk. It was a weird and not very hilarious carnival. Youths of both sexes paraded the streets making hideously discordant noises with paper trumpets, or singing snatches of pantomime choruses manufactured in Cockneydom.

The Scotch drink and the imported vulgarity did not make a pleasing blend. Otherwise it was a fairly sober and decorous crowd, sombre rather than gay, solid and stolid, unemotional on the surface, whatever it might be deeper down; impressive by sheer weight of numbers. From the top of a car, which got jammed in the middle of the crowd, I looked down on the vast multitude stretching away in all directions. Along the Trongate into Argyle Street, where the lights from shop windows not yet closed revealed a sea of human faces looking all the one way—towards the Cross; up the High Street, where the furthest fringe of the crowd seemed to melt into mysterious darkness; down the Saltmarket towards the river; and eastward by London Street and the Gallowgate a great concourse of humanity drawn as by a magnet to one common centre. Not a noisy crowd, when you remembered its immensity. There was little shouting, except here and there, and by fits and starts, when the youthful revellers seemed to get the upper hand. Only a deep universal, musical muttering in which was harmonised the articulations of some fifty thousand human throats. Oaths, obscenities, jocularities, banterings, costers' cries, lovers' talk and friendly greetings, songs and laughter, and cursings, all mixed in one great wave of sound pitched in a minor key, and sad rather than joyful.

If the question had been put—"What came ye out for to see?" I fear no very intelligible answer would have been forthcoming from any one in that great gathering. For myself, I had come out to see the crowd. Every other person to whom I spoke said that he had only come out "to see the crowd." But that was mere shame-faced self-deception. It is not reasonable to suppose that all these people had come out into the winter night merely to look at each other. There was some sentiment deep-rooted in tradition and custom, and in the human heart itself, which had brought them together. I think—I may be wrong—it was the sentiment of brotherhood. The kinship of humanity, for one brief hour, become conscious. The sense of equality, for a little space, asserting itself. In all that multifarious assemblage, no man was a stranger to any other man. *They knew each other;* though they might not have met before and might never meet again. They wished each other a happy New Year, and did so in all sincerity. A few hours hence, they might, by force of circumstances, be compelled to make the year as unhappy as possible for each other, but in this one moment the predominant feeling was goodwill, and whether expressed in sober sanity, in boisterous exuberance, or in maudlin whiskyfied incoherence, the goodwill was there: the one great eternal fact that binds us all together, makes existence endurable, and progress possible.

It is this fact, exemplified every day in some individual lives, and once a year universally, that gives assurance of the ultimate triumph of Socialism. There is a basic goodness in human nature which must make itself manifest in some way or other, whether the occasion be the nativity of the Nazarene, or, as Elia puts it, of "Our Common Adam."

Human beings do not hate each other naturally, nor take pleasure in each other's pain.

Stripped of the commercialised environment which creates social antagonisms and distinctions, life would become in reality what we actually desire it to be when we wish each other a happy New Year.

True it is that our mode of greeting has become stereotyped and commonplace. The same old handshake, the same "Happy New Year," or "Merry Christmas," as sure and certain as the festival day dawns. But therein lies the proof at once of its spontaneity and its antiquity. It is ever new and ever old.

The annual springing of a gracious flower of goodwill, having its roots in the remote beginnings of mankind on the natal day of Father Adam himself. A flower which, given the right conditions, would bloom perennially, not once a year, but all the year.

So we express the same wish in the same old way.

For how can a man say anything new about that which, though new-born to-morrow, is as old as Time itself? The year has come nigh to a close, like all the years that have gone before it, and we are repeating the same sayings and thinking the same thoughts that men and women have been saying and thinking at the endings and beginnings of years through all The Ages.

Regrets, hopes, fears, and good resolves. Burying the past that will not be buried; shaping the future that will shape itself quite otherwise than as we may plan. We have been foolish, now we shall be wise; we have been thriftless, now we shall be careful; we have been selfish, now we shall be loving and generous.

The world has gone wrong; now, now we shall set it right. The old year is done with, the new year is in sight. A Happy New Year! All years are to be happy new years. "Man never is but always to be blest," and next December those of us who are still alive will be once more burying the old and welcoming the new, cursing our past stupidities, lamenting our lost opportunities, and building another fair fabric of brave resolutions. Well, why not? Why shouldn't we periodically renew our moral armour and burnish up our swords that have grown rusty? They will grow rusty once more, all too soon, but at least let us have them bright and clean once in a while.

And why should I fear to repeat in this little book of mine the things that have been repeated a million times before? Why this craving to be original; this dread of the commonplace? The commonplace! The earth itself is a commonplace. The sun, moon, and stars are commonplace; the green grass, the blue skies, the stately trees, the lofty hills, the mountains and the valleys, the seven seas and the winds of heaven, they are all commonplace. They are thus all the time. And why should we, who by the light of the common sun and moon sail to and fro upon these common seas, and run hither and thither about this common earth, and shall all ere long sleep quietly and commonly enough in its bosom—why should we strive to be uncommon? It is a vain endeavour. It is true to-day as in the days of the wise, old commonplace king. "There is no new thing under the sun," only a different embellishment of the things that are old and common, and, therefore, precious and true.

Strange talk this from a Socialist! Well, I shall be prepared to justify it, nor yet forsake my Socialism, which is simply a new word for a very old thing—the thing which we otherwise call justice. "Common Justice." You have heard these words before.

These many, many years now the generations of men have been striving so hard to be uncommon and original that they have well-nigh forgotten about common justice. In their desire to be original they have found many substitutes and makeshifts for justice. Generosity, benevolence, philanthropy, charity. All good in their way; useful enough virtues when rightly understood and properly assorted, but arrant frauds when masquerading as justice. The earth is commonplace; Nature is commonplace; but man seeking to be original, and therefore greater than Nature, has invented artificiality. For the common inheritance of the earth he has substituted landlordism; for common ownership he has substituted private ownership. He has taken a man here and a man there and called him king, and he has taken other men here and other men there and called them lords. Others he has named capitalists or employers of labour; the common multitude of the people, those he has called hewers of wood and drawers of water. WORKERS. These latter are the *common people.* The others are the uncommon people; the improvements upon nature, the outcome of man's strivings to be original. They are greater than God. Indeed, after their own image they have made God, which is perhaps the supreme triumph of human originality over the Divinely commonplace.

Out of all this has arisen injustice, and that highly original but wholly inadequate homage to humanity's sense of morality which calls itself *Charity.* We do not want charity. We want justice. We want to get back to the commonplace, back to Nature, and strange as it may seem, we can only get this by going forward to Socialism, for Socialism is simply Nature's law of justice applied to the complexities of modern life.

When men meet each other in the streets and shake each other by the hand, this is what they mean—justice between man and man.

They do not say it like that. They say "A Happy New Year," and they mean it, and they know full well that there can be no really happy new year for any human being whilst injustice prevails. They may not have defined to themselves any clear idea as to what constitutes justice. But they want to do justly and to be justly done by in the coming year. Once a year they are brought near to each other and realise the old commonplace verity of common brotherhood.

For one little day they cease striving to be original, and clever, and uncommon; the one man bigger and better than the other man. They are "A' John Tamson's bairns." It is the involuntary vindication of the ethics of Socialism. The one-day triumph of a natural human relationship which Socialism would establish in perpetuity.

A Scottish Folksong

What shall I give you? Shall I put you off with some "auld wife's tale," or with the lilt of an "auld Scot's sang"? Perhaps with both; for there is in my ear just now the haunting tune of a sweet old song that has behind it the strange story of an Ishmaelitish woman.

Coming up through the crowded Gorbals this afternoon I heard it on the lips of a street singer:

> Ca' the ewes to the knowes,
> Ca' them where the heather grows,
> Ca' them where the burnie rows,
> My bonnie dearie.

The mockery of it! and the pathos and the tragedy of it! The sordid reeking thoroughfares; the thronging tumultuous mob; the wide-open drink-shop door, and on its threshold this woman with the tattered shawl, and the bleared face, and the broken, quivering voice; and on her lips the song of the solitudes and the moorlands, and of love stronger than death.

> While waters wimple to the sea,
> While day blinks in the lift sae hie,
> Till clay cauld death shall blin' my e'e,
> Ye shall be my dearie.

Heard ye ever anything simpler, sweeter, and truer than that? There is a singing cadence in the very words. The very essence of melody. They seem to sing themselves. And can you guess what kind of woman wrote that song—for it is a woman's song? Can you guess that it was a woman akin in fortune to her whom I heard ranting it this afternoon on Glasgow streets? Yet it was even so. This tender lyric came from the heart of one who was an outcast and a wastrel from *before the day of her birth,* and all through her life; one upon whom Nature itself had set the seal of outlawry; a woman deformed in body, and rebellious and cankered in spirit, and whose life was one long scornful defiant laugh at the conventional narrow world in which her fate was cast; a world at once wide and free as the moorland winds, and narrow and crabbed as the creed of Calvin. Wild Tibbie Pagan of Muirkirk. She lived her life in the century before last, and she rests quietly this long time in the Auld Kirkyard of Muirkirk. And even on her tombstone they were fain to make apology for her, these douce and decorous rural contemporaries at whose "even-gaun" virtues she mocked and railed.

> Interred here a votaress of mirth,
> Congenial mingling with her parent earth,
> Forgotten lies; whose wild, eccentric life
> Seemed vice and virtue in perpetual strife.
> But cease, ye mild to blame, ye prudes to sneer,
> Nought worthy praise or blame inhabits here;
> 'Tis only dust, the immortal part is gone
> To meet its just reward, in some fair world unknown.

"A votaress of mirth!"

"Vice and virtue in perpetual strife!"

Ay! but the woman of whom these words were written does not "forgotten lie." While the Scottish heart responds to melody, while the Scottish tongue lives, so long will live Isobel Pagan.

For this is a folk-song. It is the kind of song that mithers croon to the bairns in their cradles, and it gets into the very fibre of them, and the very echoes of it in a street minstrel's voice awakens old memories and the vision of a day that is gone. Guid-wives hum it as they go about their household duties, and forget their daily "cark and care," and shepherd lads whistle it as they watch their flocks, and peasant lassies keep tryst to its tune in the gloamin'.

> As I gaed doon the waterside
> There I met my shepherd lad,
> He rowed me sweetly in his plaid,
> And ca'ed me his dearie.

It is a folk-song. A song of the common folk. Of a life that has not entirely passed away and may yet come back again. Perchance, when we shall have thrown off the nightmare of commercialism, when we shall have escaped from the mechanical Bedlam which enmeshes us, we shall one day re-enter the old pastoral world to the tune of Tibbie Pagan's song, and

Ca' the ewes to the knowes,
Ca' them where the heather grows,
Ca' them where the burnie rows,
My bonnie dearie.

And who was Tibbie Pagan? Who can tell? I have told you all that I know: all that anybody knows. There is no written history of her. She lives in this song and in another love-breathing pastoral, "The Crook and the Plaid," and in the traditions of an Ayrshire country-side. The bye-blaw perchance of some roystering Ayrshire laird! "Little is known of her early life. Taken care of by an old woman, who taught her to read, she improved herself in her sparc hours," so says one local chronicler who himself has gathered his information merely from transmitted gossip. A woman cursed from the beginning. Look at this portrait of her: "Her appearance was unprepossessing. She was lame, had a squint, and a large tumour on her side." A woman formed not to be loved. Yet she sang a song of love as if Cupid himself had been her boon companion.

Ye shall get gowns and ribbons meet,
Cauf leather shoon for thy white feet,
And in my airms ye's lie and sleep,
And ye shall be my dearie.

The "gowns and ribbons meet" were not for Tibbie Pagan, and she hirpled through four score years of life, more feared than loved by her decent but unimaginative neighbours.

For with the gift of rhyme she had also the gift of sarcasm, of which she made a shield and buckler against all who dared to mock her physical infirmities, or who ventured to upbraid her moral delinquencies. For she was no saint, Tibbie Pagan. In her crooked body there dwelt a merry heart and a rebel soul, and she lampooned her enemies in satirical ballads, and carried her shafts of wit from door to door. A queer offshoot this of the race of troubadours. Had she lived a century earlier they'd have burnt her for a witch. Had she lived in Paris at the right period of history she would have queened it over some literary salon. As it was, she held a kind of court of her own right there in this remote country parish among the Ayrshire moors, in that curious dwelling of hers, made out of the end of an old brick-kiln, by the side of the Garpel Water. If she was not bonnie to look upon, she had wit and humour, and a certain de'il-may-carishness, and she sang like a lark; and all the wits and wags and roystering blades; all the rattling, roaring Willies of the country round came with their fiddles and their pipes and their gill stoups and their rough songs and rougher humours, and held high revel night after night for many a long year in the shieling of Tibbie Pagan. The memories of those wild nights hover about the hillsides to this day, and the bridge that spans the Garpel Water is "Tibbie Pagan's Brig." But these memories, too, will die; the traditions will fade away; the stories about Tibbie Pagan will be forgotten, and the old brig will crumble and fall, and when all this has come to pass, Tibbie's song will still live, and Scottish mothers in the hills and glens will still be singing to the bairns:

Ca' the ewes to the knowes,
Ca' them where the heather grows,
Ca' them where the burnie rows,
My bonnie dearie.

The Man with the Whistle

He stood in front of a public house in a quiet street of a quiet town, and played most heart-rendingly upon a penny whistle. It was the bleakest, rawest, cruellest day in March, and the merciless wind made mocking sport through the holes of his shabby overcoat, which vainly endeavoured to conceal the absence of coat or waistcoat underneath.

It was the time of day when few people are about; when the men are at work, and the children are at school, and the women folks are reddin' up, and audience he had none, except one solitary one-eyed mongrel dog that sat in front of him, looking appealingly sideways, but without energy enough to howl a protest. He had a most comprehensive repertoire, and I think he went right through it. Grave and gay, merry and sad, hopeful, and despairing, but never a soul came to listen, or to give him anything; not even a policeman to tell him to go away. It was too cold. Yet he would not give in. He whistled "Nil Desperandum" and "Home, Sweet Home." The wind carried the strains of "Soldiers of the Queen," half a mile away, but nobody came. Neither Annie Laurie nor Annie Rooney had charms to attract a solitary admirer.

He played jigs, strathspeys, and hornpipes, and merry marching tunes, but all in vain. He was a brave man.

But even the bravest must own defeat sometimes, and the most long-winded "hold their breath, for a time." Only for a time, however. He put his whistle in his pocket, stuck his hat more firmly on his head, and lifted up his voice—and sang. Most appallingly! His power of lung was amazing; his method of vocalisation original; declamatory dramatic, and devil-may-care, a kind of cross between an operatic tenor and an auctioneer. The effect was instantaneous. The one-eyed dog turned tail and fled, people opened their windows and looked out, wondering what the Salvation Army was doing abroad at this time of day. " 'Twill be all right to-morrow," he sang, " 'Twill be all right to-morrow, 'twill be all right to-morrow, though it's all gone wrong to-day."

The pathetic optimism of the unlucky. The vagrant's defiance of time and fate and circumstance! To-morrow, and to-morrow, and evermore to-morrow. 'Twill be all the same a hundred years hence. A couple of navvies came out of the public house. "Say, mate," said one of them, "that's a cold job you've got; come inside and wet your whistle." His philosophy had vindicated itself. To-morrow had come sooner than he expected. The singer's voice was hushed, and a great silence fell upon that quiet street in that quiet town.

That was two and a half years ago. Several times I have met him since then in various parts of the country, and every time it was in front of tavern doors. But let not the ultra-respectable reader contrive out of that coincidence anything derogatory to the character either of the man with the whistle or of the present writer. It was mere coincidence, I assure you; and is not all human history mainly a matter of coincidence? Only last week I spied him again at the portals of Rutherford's in the Gallowgate piping up the same old tunes, with the same imperturbable front of indifference to his environment.

I confess to a liking for my whistling wastrel. He is not an ornamental member of society certainly, nor a useful, in the utilitarian sense, and his philosophy, if he has any, is that of Thackeray's Idler, "nothing's new or true, and it doesn't matter." It is a false philosophy, no doubt, but it is the creed of modern society, and it has been thrust upon him, and he finds it workable. If he has lost hope, he has also conquered fear, neither rent-collector nor tax-gatherer can worry *him;* nor any overseer cause him to tremble. He has lost his respectability and gained his freedom; and thus, an honest rogue, and idle vagabond, he goes whistling by devious paths towards to-morrow, which, when it dawns for the last time, will probably find him on the sheltered side of a hedge, with his face turned up to the sky, silently proclaiming once for all that "it doesn't matter."

There are many such as he: hundreds, thousands. The number of them is ever increasing, and, strange though it may seem, some of you who, with a certain complacent sympathy, read this slight sketch will yourselves be forced one day to join the strolling company. This is no mere surmise. It is an absolute certainty. It is written in the book of fate, whose name is *competition,* that some of you, for as well settled as you seem to be, will be competed out of your present respectable but uncomfortable ways of life, and into the ranks of the unemployed, from whom are recruited the roving race of vagabonds whom ye are apt to despise. You will be no longer needed in the world of labour. There will be no abiding place for you in your "ain countree." You will furbish up your penny whistles and other instruments of torture and make tracks into the free world of vagrancy, and probably you will not be more miserable then than the most of you are at the present time. Every depression of trade, every new invention, every strike or lock-out sends more men and women on the road never to look back again to the old humdrum methods of wearing out life, and so it will be while the present system continues. I point no moral, I preach no sermon, I proclaim no remedy. I leave that to the philosophers, the preachers, and the statesmen, but I hope they will not forget that the man with the whistle is quite as much a part of the problem they have to face as the man with the hoe, or the man with the bank book.

A Border Raid

I have just paid my first visit to the Borderland. Merely a fleeting visit. Merely a railway rush through the hills, a day and a night's sojourn amongst the folk of Hawick, and then a rush back through the hills once more to the smoke and fog and bustle of the city. No more than a glimpse of the enchanted land, but sufficient to awaken a thousand memories. For though it is my first visit in the flesh, in fancy I have been there many and many a time. Long, long years ago, ere life had revealed to me its prosaic reality, I walked the border road to Edinburgh with a man in hodden grey, Dandie Dinmont by name. I think I met him on Saturday in Hawick. He turned to whistle his terriers to heel, but it was a collie that answered the call, and perhaps it was not Dandie Dinmont at all I met, but the shepherd of Ettrick Vale. I knew him, too, in that olden time, and many jovial noctes I held with him and Christopher North, and Walter Scott, and all that jolly fellowship of hard drinkers, high thinkers, and merry singers.

And even before that I had been to the borders, and had lifted the Englishman's kye on many a moonlight night with Wat o' Harden, and Kinmont Willie, and Jamie Telfer, and Johnny Armstrong, and had nursed dark thoughts of revenge for Flodden Field. Yes; and I had danced with the elves and fairies on the Eildon Hills. So, though it was my first visit, I was no stranger in a strange land. And my journey through the hills was not altogether disenchantment. The social conditions have been modernised, and the Border men no longer ride to feud and foray on moonlight nights, and the factory system has taken possession of some of the fairest valleys, but the hills are there as of old. You may modernise humanity, but you cannot modernise the everlasting hills. Even a factory on a mountain side takes unto itself some of the majesty of its environment and becomes clothed in a kind of mystic beauty. If you have imagination enough you can turn it into a kind of Robber's Castle. "And that is what it really is," I hear some matter-of-fact Socialist say. But I am not having any matter of fact at present. It may be true what you say, that the factory lords are simply robbers, like the "Bauld Buccleuch" and the "Black Douglas" in the old raiding days. It may be true, what you say, that the factory hands are merely the Buccleuch's serfs brought up-to-date, but I am not going to let you spoil my journey into the enchanted country with your Socialistic theorisings and economics.

The hills are there, white and soft and wonderful under their covering of snow, and I am quite sure that on the Eildon summits the faires are playing their pranks. And if not the faires, then the witches and warlocks. It is just a night to their liking. The wind is making weird music through the valleys, and the voices of the rushing, swollen streams give answer. The snowflakes are dancing demoniacally 'twixt earth and heaven, and fantastic, ghostly shapes are forming themselves in the ravines and in the clefts of the hills.

Why, it was on just such a night as this that we rescued Kinmont Willie from Carlisle Keep. Do you remember?

And when we left the Staneshaw bank,
The wind began full loud to blaw,
But 'twas wind and weet, and fire and sleet,
When we came beneath the castle wa'.

And do you remember how we swam the Eden water, and petrified the Englishmen?

He is either himsel' a devil frae hell,
Or else his mother a witch maun be;
I wadna have ridden that wan water
For a' the gowd in Christendtie.

Don't talk to me of your twentieth century, with its

steam, and its electricity, and its motor-cars, and its city slums, and its Liberal and Tory parties. Was not that Fair Melrose Abbey we passed just now, where the Abbot and his jolly friars are supping bravely on fat capons and good red wine?

There is no twentieth century. There are no city slums. There are no Liberals and Tories. There are only Monks on the one hand and Puritans on the other; and on either side of the Border, raiders and cattle lifters; and though the common folk may be serfs, they do not any of them starve, nor travel from town to town seeking what master may buy them. No, I won't have your twentieth century. I have come to the Border Land, and it is still the Border Land of the days of old.

And, indeed, it is not so very difficult, after all, to rebuild this world of fancy. I have been to Lanarkshire and to Ayrshire, and have tried sometimes to live over again the days of the Covenanters, or to plough the fields with Robert Burns.

But there are coal-pits in Lanarkshire and Ayrshire, and somehow coal-pits don't fit in with poetic peasants and stern Covenant men.

There are no coal-pits on the Border Land, and though the factory system is here, it has not yet got down to the making of shoddy. It has not yet defiled the streams and rivers. Teviot and Gala water still run clear and free; along their banks the birds still build their nests, and the trout and salmon have not yet been poisoned. The factory smoke is not yet so thick as to darken the sky or kill the wild flowers or taint the mountain air, and even something of the old border spirit still lives in the hearts of the people. They go poaching now and then, and defy the powers that be. And I have an idea—perhaps it is only fancy, like all that I have here written—that this same border spirit will be strong and virile enough to save this bonnie country side from ever being entirely conquered and devastated by commercialism.

They are the same people who, through long generations, held the debatable land against the English foe. They are here still, the Elliotts, and Armstrongs, and Scotts, and Riddells, and Laidlaws. Perhaps when they understand the nature of the enemy that now invades their hills and dales, and assails their liberties, they will fight as effectively with the vote as their fathers did with the sword; and if they should invest the struggle with some of that romance and poesy which lingers still round every Border hillside, that will be all to the good. A little sentiment, chivalry, idealism, call it what you will, can do the Labour movement no harm. I wish somebody would write us a song like "March! March! Ettrick and Teviotdale." It would do us more good than a whole armoury of statistics.

If any matter-of-fact friend says "Rubbish," well let him. I have been to the Border Land, and I am proof against that kind of sarcasm.

A Highland Glen

I am no artist in scenery, and there are emotions aroused by nature's contact which may be felt but cannot be transmitted.

Yet, I shall not soon forget the sense of exhilaration that thrilled me when on a "bright May morning early" I found myself walking the further shore of Loch Long. An hour previous we had left the city, just as it was waking from its slumbers, with sleepy-eyed workmen hurrying in all directions to their daily toil; and here we were in the heart of the solitudes, watching the gulls fishing for their breakfast, listening to the myriad birds chirping their love-songs, and to the blended murmuring of many streams rushing from the hills, among whose precipices far up towards the clouds could be seen those same streams glistening white and silvery like jewels on a rugged background of bare, brown rock, and indistinguishable almost from the creviced snow patches not yet melted by the summer sun. The way lies in amongst these hills, and to the man from the town every step seems like a step into the land of mystery. He follows the course of the Croe Burn, descending as he ascends. Along a path at first bordered on either side by bushes of whin bearing a lusty wealth of golden flower, but becoming more and more barren as it recedes from the shore of the loch. Hither and thither, deviously and windingly, goes the path, but always and ever upward. And the higher you ascend the loftier still stand up the great mountains in front of you. To right and left of you also they stand, and now as you turn to look back the way you came, lo! there also are the mountains. You are surrounded; you are shut in; you are in the midst of a great hill-encircled glen. Outside of that ring of hills lies the world of men and commerce. You know that it is there—you left it only a little while ago. But now—now—it is over the hills and far, far away. The world you have left is the world of fable and phantasy. This is the real world, and it is not a world of human beings. Among these straggling pines and scraggy rocks and mountain cliffs the birds of the air have their nests and the foxes have their holes; but the son of man! This is no place for him. Yet it was not always so. All the way up the glen, and on either side, there lie the crumbling ruins of human homesteads, not easily discernible, for long ago they have assimilated in colour to the brown rocks of which they now seem to be part. Once upon a time there was here, even amongst these lonesome hills, a community of human beings. Here was crofters' land, and the laughter of healthy Hieland bairns echoed to the song of the birds and the burn. In all these six miles up the glen we have met only three human beings, and these were children from the shepherd's cot in the valley corner, tripping barefoot along the burnside towards a rabbit-hutch sort of little schoolhouse, where I suppose some itinerant dominie meets them daily to impart instruction. Here is a quaint aspect of the education problem. The teaching of these two or three bairns must be more costly than that of hundreds in more populous places.

The crofters have gone overseas to Canada, or up the Clyde to the Glasgow slums. The sheep and the shepherd have taken their place. There is nothing left of the hillside shielings but the scattered stones of which they were built.

Sun Worship

Summer has come. I know, for I have been to look for it. East to north I went in search of it, but it was in the west I found it. Summer enters royally through the western gate. On Sunday last I saw the sun sink in the sea where it is softly shadowed by the Arran hills. It was the *summer sun*. It was no case of mistaken identity. The winds were warm with the breath of him, and odorous with the perfumes he had charmed from earth and sea. The skies were rich with the glow of his artistry. All day long he had caressed the hills and the valleys, as if he loved them. And now, slowly and reluctantly he left us; nay, he did not altogether leave us, for his shimmering afterlight remained, the night air quivered in uncertain radiance, and lengthened the gloaming hour into the morning; and ere we knew that the sun had left us, lo! he was with us once again, bidding the sons and daughters of men to lift up their hearts and rejoice, and be merry and glad, for that of a very truth the summer was here, with its beneficence and blessing.

And the sons and daughters of men, with their usual perversity, went and did the very opposite. For just at the hour when the refreshing morning sun was shining forth his kindliest rays, they went, some millions of them, and immured themselves in factories, and tied themselves to machines, and even themselves became like unto the machines, or as sticks and stones that know neither heat nor cold; and they tried to hide themselves from the light of the sun; and others bound themselves to desks in places called counting-houses, and buried their noses in ledgers and turned the backs of their necks and the bald places of their craniums to the sun; and others there were who ran away from the sun altogether, and descended into the bowels of the earth, into coal-mines and quarry holes and dark foulsome corners, where the sun never penetrates. And they would have nothing to do with the sun, any more than if he were their mortal enemy. Some of them even, who did not go into factories, or mines, or counting-houses, covered themselves with parasols, illuminated with brilliant colours, stolen from the very sun whom they had rejected.

And the sun, in his anger at the perversity of all these ridiculous people, shot down the lances and shafts of his wrath through the glass windows of their factories and counting-houses, and burnt the backs of their necks, and frizzled the bald spots on their heads, and scorched and roasted and tormented them, until they sweated and cursed and swore, and said it was "an awfu' hot summer!" And he descended into their coal-mines and played tricks with their oxygen, and there were explosions and accidents, and these people, too, said it was "an awfu' hot summer!" As for the persons underneath the parasols, to them he did nothing at all. He could not make them any worse, or more ridiculous than they already were.

For me, I did not go into any of their factories, nor counting-houses, nor coal-mines—but I did what was quite as bad. Like a born fool, I stuck myself into a crowded railway train, crammed full of other born fools, all fleeing with express speed from the seashore and the yellow sands, and the woodland greenery and the summer sun. Fleeing into the city. We couldn't get there quick enough. None of your slow-going trains for us, lingering leisurely on the way and stopping at all the pleasant wayside stations. In hot haste all of us to get into the city, where even the good, kind sun turns traitor and leagues himself with the tyrant and the oppressor; where the very air smells rank to Heaven; where the pavement beneath your feet is like unto a furnace seven times heated; where the sprawling ragged children look up piteously at you from their closes and corners, like condemned sprites in a demon-enchanted Hades; and where the business men go chasing their dividends and hugging their cares, and jostling and pushing and driving, and grinning diabolically to each other, "It's an awfu' hot summer!" The fools! As if they knew anything about the summer! And fools we, who have come in amongst them! Fools, all of us, who allow ourselves to be defrauded of any of the joy of living!

These utterances of mine, you say, are but the petulant whimsicalities of a discontented dreamer. You are wrong. They are the expressions of a reasonable discontent, that lies at the heart of every rational human being in these beautiful summer days. And if there be a dream behind them, it is a dream that will yet come true. I expect, when the Socialist Party grows strong enough, they will bring in a Bill to nationalise the summer, and it will be carried *nemine contradicente.* And in the cool hours of the early summer morning we shall all do our three hours' pleasant work for the common weal; and humanity, for the first time since the invention of the factory system, will be free to live. And in those days when the sun goes down behind the hills of Arran, it will be to rise, not upon a mad world with its back turned towards him, but upon a world of sun-worshippers, paying joyous homage to the source of life and light.

The Philosophy of Holidays

At this time of the year it is in order to write about holidays and holiday-makers, and who so fit to do so as the man who hasn't been having any? Just as the onlooker sees most of the game, so the man who stays at home while the rest of the world goes wandering may, if he have only a little sympathetic imagination, and be not too much bitten by the canker-worm of envy, find a whole world of enjoyment in the pleasures of other people. I have this year been to Skye, and St. Kilda, and the Isle of Man, and London, and Paris, and the Trossachs, and the Anglo-French Exhibition, yet never stirred a peg from home.

The home-keeping holiday-maker becomes a kind of human reception-house for the holiday impressions of all his wayfaring friends. To him come glowing letters a' the airts the wind can blaw, with sprigs of heather from the north and rose leaves from the sunny south, and weirdly descriptive accounts of Elysian fields, where there are neither workshops, nor factories, nor slums, nor counting-houses, nor ledgers; and where the wicked cease from troubling and the weary are at rest—for the space of a whole fortnight. To him also, as by the impetus of some natural law, come those home-returning braves, the sun-browned Munchausens in fantastic cycling attire, brimming over with tantalising fairy tales of strange adventures by flood and field, Clarion Campers, Ruskin Fellowshippers, Cook's Excursionists—the whole crowd of them, not in single spies merely, but in whole battalions, making it a point to seek out the man who hasn't been anywhere, and in a spirit of purest altruistic benevolence — some call it malevolence — regaling him with celestial glimpses of the unattainable.

Yet not perhaps the wholly unattainable either, for he has only to pull on those fabulous seven-league boots, which are a part of the essential outfit of every true dreamer, and, hey, presto! he, too, goes a-roving by hill and dale and forest, "by wells and rills and meadows green."

And he has this advantage, that he views the world in its merriest mood, through other eyes than his own, through the myriad eyes of the whole crowd of holiday-makers, who, leaving the factory system behind them as if it had never been, are, like Eugene Aram's juvenile friends, bent on turning to mirth all things of earth, and making life itself "a thing of beauty and a joy," as I have said, for a whole blooming fourteen days. It is a great and significant fact this annual holiday-making. Once a year every soul of us who can afford it must be on the move. Even the slum dwellers, wherever possible, obey what seems to be a natural instinct. The Glasgow newsboy will be found selling song sheets at Paisley or Hamilton races, just for a change of air and scene, and at quiet country fairs you will meet with the leather-lace merchant of Cathedral Square busily plying his trade.

I seem to discern in the natural avidity with which we all take to the road the doom of the seemingly immutable factory system, and the proof that it is at variance with natural law. The other day I met a man who, in his brief spell of freedom, had cycled seven hundred miles. He had been up among the Hielan' hills. His talk was all of mountain passes and misty glens and roaring cataracts. He was brown and strong and sturdy. To look at him you would never have guessed that he was city born and bred, that all his working days had been spent amid the smoke and the crowds, or that he had ever known what it was to earn his bread by a daily ten hours' grind in a city workshop. But that, like the most of us, he was a bit undersized, he seemed a veritable son of the hills; so easily do we return to nature, and so quickly does nature claim us for her own, and place her stamp of kinship upon us. As with my friend, so with the rest of us. This annual rush for the open air and the free life, be it only for a few days, or even for a few hours, is humanity's protest against the artificiality of modern conditions—an unconscious protest for the most part, but all the more significant because of its spontaneity. We may not all of us turn to the hills like my cycling friend. Many of us have not energy enough left for that, and a quiet spot suffices us, where we may simply rest and draw breath freely for a little space, and call our souls our own. We are apt to go in crowds, most of us, just to keep each other in countenance in our childish abandonment to the unwonted delights of liberty. But what we are all seeking, and must have, if we are to live, is escape, however brief, from the prison-house of Commercialism, which we have dignified by the name of an industrial system. This, I think, is the whole philosophy of modern holiday-making, and whether we spend our few brief days of relaxation in getting drunk, or in climbing hills, or in camping out, or, like Sandy Haddow and Tom M'Kerrell, in preaching Socialism through town and village, we are all alike in revolt, and if we have to creep back to our cages again, it is with an increased appreciation of the possibilities of life, and a renewed determination to widen and extend those possibilities until liberty shall be the normal condition of human existence, and not as now, a mere occasional privilege snatched from the weary, slow-going years of drudgery and toil.

Corn Rigs

The summer is past, the brown leaves are falling, and winter comes on apace. It is not alone the changing face of nature that reminds me of the inevitable approach of the darksome days. There is a kind of rustle and bustle of preparation in human affairs, a gathering together of committees, a compiling of syllabuses, an arranging of municipal programmes, and a selecting of municipal candidates which speak all too surely of November blasts—and counterblasts. An intimation from the secretary of the Glasgow South-side Sunday School informs me that their indoor work begins on Sunday first. There is no longer any room for doubt about it—the summer is already as a "tale that is told." Its glory is fading, and there remains but the aftermath; yet that, too, has its own charm and glory for all who have eyes to see, and ears to hear, the beauty and the music of nature.

It is the season when kindly old Mother Earth, having given forth her increase, seems resting from her labours and preparing to meet the stormy onslaughts of invading winter, whose chilling frosty heralds are already in the morning breeze, robbing the trees and the hedges of their verdure, and laying low the flowers of summer. It is the harvest time, the same kind of harvest time which Robert Burns looked upon on that immortal Lammas nicht when "corn rigs were bonnie." Corn rigs are bonnie still, and always will be, whether when the "moon is shining clearly," or when the mellow autumn sun looks contentedly down upon the rich warm fields of colour which are his own creation. On such a day I know of nothing pleasanter than to stretch yourself out with your back on a barley stook, and watch the reaping of the harvest. You must not, however, harass your conscience with any misgivings as to the morality of idling your time while other people are working, and you can always soothe yourself with the reflection that you are not the only idle man in the field. Have you ever noticed that on every harvest-field there is always one man doing nothing? The strongest man on the field, too—big and broad and burly. He could do the work of three of these women there if he were to try. But he does nothing, and says nothing. He simply stands looking on, now in this corner of the field and now in that; but wherever he stands, the reaping machine seems to go a little faster, the backs of the labourers seem to bend more assiduously to their task, and you begin to perceive that there are more ways of driving than by using a whip.

And as I lie here I think I can see another idle man. Invisible to you he may be, but he is there all the same, pacing step for step with Mr. Farmer. The landlord, he is called, this silent shadow with his hands in the other man's pocket; and the very first fruits of the harvest, the choicest sheaves, belong to him. And still another shadow figure I seem to see, dogging grimly the footsteps of the other two. Of venerable Hebraic cast of countenance this one, I think. It is from him that the farmer has borrowed what he calls his capital, and he is waiting now for his ten per cent., which the harvesters are gathering in for him this autumn afternoon.

I don't think the labourers in the fields are conscious of the presence of these other personages who appear to me so plainly. If they were they would surely do as you and I have done—lie down in the sun and rest, and leave the other three to get in the harvest themselves. It is for these three that the reaping machines go merrily to and fro and the men and women strenuously sweat and toil like automatic Titans. Rent, profit, and interest brood over all the harvest fields in Merrie England, and in the background there is Pauperism, which is perhaps represented by you and I as we lie idly looking on.

I lay at my ease on the harvest field, with my back to my stook of barley. The rays of the autumn sun caressed me as if they loved me. The south wind came softly and gently from "over the hills and far away," bearing in its breath the odours of many cornlands, and the salt strength of the sea—a mile away. And what with the sun and the wind, and the winged sounds around and about me, I just, as we Scotch people say, "dovered owre" into the land of dreams. And my dream seemed to be for the most part a kind of song; or the memory of a song. The lilting chorus of an old, old tune—

> **Bonnie lassie, will ye go? will ye go? will ye go?**
> **Bonnie lassie, will ye go, and join yon band o' shearers?**

Soft and low at first, then lustily and loud; and the field was alive with human forms; swanky, strong limbed men, and lithesome, heartsome lassies. And the swishing, sweeping play of their gleaming heuks among the yellow corn was a sight to see, the very poetry and perfection of lightsome labour; and as they toiled they sang; and as they sang they laughed; and their singing laughter went rippling down the rigs from lip to lip, like unto the rustling music of the wind among the barley. And the ripe grain went down before them, and the binders bound it lovingly into sheaves: and the barefoot gleaning laddies, with "Gavroche" among them, came prickling through the stubble as gloaming fell; and we were all happy and merry and healthy and hungry, and then—something went wrong—somebody invented something, I think. The thing he invented came too near my barley stook, and I wakened up to find my band o' shearers gone, and the harvest field deserted, save for some half-dozen worn and weary labourers, the attendant slaves to that rickety-rackety machine.

Where be they now, those bands of shearers? Reaping happy harvests in Elysian fields? I hope so. One thing I do know, there is little of laughing or singing, or joking among the forlorn band of labourers on this field where I now lie. It looks as if there were not a song in the hearts of any one of them. You cannot find any tune, new or old, that will sing to the refrain of "Rent, Profit and Interest." Yet, not even the selfishness of man can utterly destroy the loveliness of nature, and corn rigs are bonnie still. While there is loveliness on the earth, love itself must find an abiding place in some human hearts. By the power of love we shall yet win forward to the time when this land shall be our own land—when the fruits of the earth shall no longer be gambled with, nor wasted, nor hoarded, but shall be dedicated to the life and happiness of all the people.

"Mang Muirs and Mosses Mony"

Recently I had occasion to spend some time in Muirkirk, in Ayrshire.

The history of Muirkirk is an inseparable part of the history of Scottish freedom. Religious freedom, National freedom, are but resting places on the way towards that universal freedom for which Socialism strives. To me, therefore, as a Scot and as a Socialist, this old town and its surroundings had a very peculiar charm. I know not how it may be explained, but it is a fact that we who live in the hope of a better time for humanity have still an occasional strange hankering for the past. Perhaps it is the very sordidness of the present which drives us back on the time when men, if they had less refinement, had at least more sincerity, and were nearer to nature. William Morris looked both backwards and forwards, and either way he descried the vision of an Earthly Paradise.

In some degree it is the same with us all. There is an element of truth in what our enemies say of us: that we are dreamers all. As a relief from to-day's stress and toil, we turn in fancy either to the brave days of old, or to the brave days that are to come, and from both we draw strength and courage. This much we can say: our dreams of the past have once been true; our dreams of the future will yet be so. For myself, when I can get away from the artificial environment of the city, and into some quiet corner which the hustling spirit of modernity has not entirely claimed for its own, this imaginative habit of mine is strong upon me. When I am in the Scottish Highlands, the clansmen come to life again, and the slogan shrills eerily through the glens.

Set me down in any fishing village on the East Fife coast, and looking seaward, I can see driving before the wind the shining sails of the old sea-kings, from "Norraway ower the faem." And here in the ancient debatable ground betwixt Lanark and Ayr in the country of the Covenant, I seem to see the old blue banner waving once more among the muirland hills, and hear the cursing shouts of the troopers of Claverhouse, answered by the battle psalms of the Ayrshire peasants, as they make their last stand for conscience' sake.

Nor is this any extreme flight of fancy. The surrounding scenery helps the illusion. Industrialism, as yet, has little changed the aspect of this countryside. The wild mosslands, like the men reared upon them, are difficult of conquest. Here and there a coal pit lifts its gallows-like framework above the surface of the moor, but somehow in this world of brown bog and heather, these excrescences do not seem quite so hideous as when set against softer landscapes. Even the ever-growing mountain of slag thrown out by the Eglinton Ironworks is not altogether out of harmony in form and colour with the natural features of the country.

True, there is smoke and fire, such as would have seemed to the men of the Covenant times like veritable exhalations from the pit of Tophet itself, and in the quiet night time, the sough of the water-engine sounds like the forfoughten sighing of a wearied giant imprisoned in the hillside. Otherwise, the sights and sounds are much as they were two hundred years ago. The blackcock still whirrs across the heather; the Garpel and Ayr water sing through the valley as they have done from time immemorial. Ayr's Moss stretches away towards Cumnock, waste and dreary, yet mystically beautiful, just as it did on that heroic day when Cameron and his comrades fell fighting one to ten. Down in the valley, there is the spot where the ploughman lad, keeping tryst with his lass, met Death instead at the hands of the troopers. It is lonely and sheltered, and fit for lovers' meetings still. South of the Strath—I think it is south, for I am not quite sure of my airts here—Cairntable still guards the inaccessible region beyond, where the men of the Covenant so often found shelter from their enemies, and where long before the Red Douglas bade defiance to the English King. On the north side Middlefield Law keeps watch and ward, and back from that again, though unseen by us, lies Loudon Hill, where Claverhouse, the grim hunter of men, himself became the hunted, and had to flee for his life. It was up near the top of this same Strath, only a few miles from where we stand, that with his own hand he shot Brown, of Priesthill, under circumstances which have made the name of the martyr sacred, and that of the slayer for ever execrable to the Scottish people. It is, indeed, holy ground for liberty's votaries. Every bog and morass, every streamlet's ford, every old farm sheiling, has its story—legendary or historical—preserving for us the memory of that long struggle, which was in the main a war between the common people and the upper classes. What wonder if I have forgotten the utilitarian mission which brought me hither, and have lost myself in the recollection of those past days and "battles long ago."

And what wonder if we still look for great things from the dwellers in this region, whether their way of life be the old pastoral one of sheep rearing, or the more strenuous hewing of coal and puddling of iron? The memorials of past heroisms are all around them. They spend their days amidst natural surroundings that develop strength of body and mind and originality of character. For this is the land of Kyle that gave us Robert Burns. These "muirs and mosses mony" have given us many a true singer and strong fighter, and will again.

If I judge aright, they are of a race of men who will be less moved by the injustice which prescribes material poverty than by the wrong which sets limits to spiritual and political freedom, and when once they realise that under modern capitalism material poverty involves mental slavery, they will be found, not merely side by side with the rest of us, in the advanced Labour movement, *but in the van.*

The Vagrant and the Gentleman

There is a good deal of talk just now, in Parliament and out of it, about the vagrant, that perennially pathetic person who has been stravaigin about these isles for many centuries now.

A Parliamentary Commission has been considering the vagrant, and has put him into a Blue Book, not for the first nor for the hundredth time, and I notice that a certain editor anticipates, as one of the Blue Book results, the transformation of our policemen into guardian angels. That may be. I am sure I hope so. The celestialisation of Robert would be worth while. But what about the vagrant? Is it not strange that every attempt to deal with him has invariably dealt with someone else, and left him as he was before—a vagrant and a wanderer?

I don't know whether it is a good sign or not, this renewed interest in the vagrant; whether it denotes an awakened social conscience, or whether it is merely that well-to-do folk don't like the look of this everlasting Ishmaelite whose looped and windowed raggedness jars so uncouthly on their highly-developed sense of propriety. It cannot be altogether pleasant for refined ladies and gentlemen in motor-cars to be in perpetual danger of running over these tramping beggars and their starving brats. Before the motor-car came it was different. The vagrant was not in the habit of getting in the way of the express trains. But now that the gentlemen of England have themselves taken to the road it is intolerable that this poverty-stricken scarecrow of a vagrant should be allowed to get between the wind and their nobility. Don't you think so? and don't you think this may account for the otherwise inexplicable interest in the vagrant? I don't wish to be uncharitable to these Parliamentary gentlemen, but it does appear as if their chief concern was to get the vagrant *out of sight* rather than to deal with the causes of his existence. They want to take him off the road; to shut him up in Labour Colonies and Settlements, probationary and otherwise. He will be safe there, and he won't be in any danger of being run over by rich men's motor-cars; and he can die there just as comfortably as at the back of a hedge. That seems to be the idea. Above all, they want to make him work. That is the great objection to the vagrant, so they say; he won't work; and as that is one of the characteristics in which the gentlemen of England think they should have a monopoly, they naturally object to this shameless competitor. Which is very inconsistent on their part when you reflect that they haven't any work to give him.

They haven't work to give even to the foolish people who are anxious to work, and so they have what they call an "unemployed problem." And if that is so, what is the use of asking the vagrant to work? It is as unreasonable as if you were to ask the gentlemen of England themselves to take off their coats. They don't seem to understand the kinship there is between the gentleman and the vagrant.

I wonder what would happen if some day all the hundreds of thousands of vagrants in the British Isles made up their minds that they wanted to work; that they would *have* work; that they *must* have work. I fear it would be a bad day for the gentlemen. That, however, is too painful an aspect of the subject for continued contemplation. Besides, it implies a contingency that is not likely to happen for a long time to come, and there will be a few hundred more Parliamentary Commissions before it arrives. When it does come it will be as the result not merely of a change in human nature, but of a change in our entire social system. There will then be neither vagrants nor gentlemen, but only citizens; though the roving desire that is in every healthy man's blood will then probably find freer scope than it does now, and tramping men will take the road fearless of either motor-cars, penal settlements, or policemen.

Meantime, I want to ask, at the risk of offending some of my most intimate and upright and politically economic friends, Why should it be considered a crime for any man not to be willing to work? Has anybody ever known anybody—not an idiot—who was willing to work? Doesn't every sane man look forward to the time when he won't require to work? That is why he works—to escape from work. That is the normal ideal. Two men have realised it—the gentleman and the vagrant. You take off your hats to the gentleman. I take off mine to the vagrant. The gentlemen want to suppress him. I say, more power to him. May he live and flourish and multiply and overspread the land, and become so much of an intolerable nuisance to the gentlemen that honest folk will find it necessary to get rid of them both. But while we tolerate the idle gentleman, I hold that we have no right to interfere with the idle vagrant. If you don't like my logic, you can prove that it is wrong, and I think you will not find that an easy matter.

The vagrant is not going to be cleared off the roads for some time to come, and certainly not by the methods suggested by the Vagrancy Commissioners. These gentlemen have invented an admirable and highly ingenious plan which has only one defect. It won't work. It takes no account of human nature, and it wholly ignores the influence of modern economic developments.

First of all, this plan appeals to the charitable to cease being charitable. Kind-hearted people are to button up their pockets and steel their hearts against every tale of distress and to withhold the cup of cold water even from the least of these outcasts of society. Thus the tramping vagrants and sturdy beggars are to be "rounded up," so to speak, and driven into the arms of the angelic policeman, to be handed over to the tender mercies of the penal settlement. It is a beautiful plan, but it won't work. It will break down at both ends. Goodhearted folk who have a copper to spare will continue to help the lame dog over the stile without taking time to sit in judgment upon his sins. And when you have filled your settlements and workhouses, what are you going to do then? Have you forgot that you have an industrial system which is specially constructed and adapted for the perpetual manufacture of vagrants—and gentlemen? The first man of science who comes along with a good labour-saving invention will turn you out more ready-made vagrants in one year than your labour colonies can deal with in fifty. No, good friends, it won't do. There is only one cure for vagrancy, and that is to *stop making vagrants.* You may wriggle and dodge and shirk the issue as much as you please, but "to that complexion you must come at last." When once you turn your attention seriously to that aspect of the question there will be some hope that the idle vagrant may disappear. But don't forget this. When he goes, the idle gentleman will go along with him. Who said Socialism?

Carnegieism

In olden times there used to be in the philosophy of humble folk a mysterious kind of beneficent force which went by the name of Providence.

"Confide ye aye in Providence, for Providence is kind," sang one homely Scotch bard even before Browning had made the optimistic discovery that "God's in his heaven, all's right with the world."

That, however, was before the days of the American Steel Trust, and neither the domestic Ballantine nor the transcendental Browning could have foreseen that Providence would be superseded by Andrew Carnegie.

Yet so it has come to pass. Mr. Carnegie, after a life spent in "gathering gear by every wile that's justified" by the commercial code of honour, has now set up as an angel of "sweetness and light," and Providence is finally deposed. When we want anything nowadays which we can't get by our own efforts we turn instinctively to Mr. Carnegie, and the model millionaire never fails us, or hardly ever. Whether it be a free library, a swimming bath, a university endowment, a public park, a church organ, or advice on the tariff question, it comes all right—free, gratis, and for nothing, like "manna" from heaven. The "toiling masses" are relieved of all care, worry, and responsibility. They have nothing to do but *keep on toiling*, secure in the knowledge that the gifts of the latter-day gods will arrive in due course, via Pittsburg, New York, and Skibo.

Seriously, Mr. Carnegie's munificence raises ethical, civic, and political questions of great importance in the formation both of individual and national character. He would be a churl indeed who would deny to Mr. Carnegie the credit of good intentions, or who would fail to acknowledge that he is striving to do good with this extraordinary superfluity of wealth over which he has gained control.

But when that has been said, there remains a humiliating sense of the demoralising absurdity of the relations between Mr. Carnegie and the recipients of his bounty. Why should it be in the power of any one man, or any class of men, to give or to withhold sweetness and light? and why should any self-respecting community be proud to accept as gifts those privileges and rights, the very acceptance of which, at the hands of a private individual, are a confession either of communal incapacity or of communal pauperism, or of both? Mr. Carnegie has written of Triumphant Democracy. It has been left for him, even through his munificence, to show us Democracy abased. If we want parks and libraries and university education, we ought to be able to get these things for ourselves; and we would be able to get them for ourselves were it not that the means for getting them is appropriated by such men as Mr. Carnegie. The fault, of course, lies not with the Carnegies, but with the industrial system which makes the appropriation possible, but it is a proof of how little the elementary principle of democracy is yet understood that whole communities can accept what is little else than wholesale charity and still not be affronted.

Yet this is becoming one of the outstanding features of modern civic life. It is one of the methods by which rich men seek to achieve immortality.

There are Elder Parks and Libraries in Govan; there are Coats Memorial Churches and Clark Memorial Halls in Paisley; and Carnegie benefactions in Dunfermline, yet in none of these places is there a superabundance of sweetness and light—nor likely to be. Men and women and children toil in factories, and thread mills, and shipyards, and foundries ten hours a day for a bare living, and find life just as hard as if there were no privately-bestowed libraries and parks and halls. They live in one-roomed or two-roomed houses, and have as much difficulty in paying the rent as ever they had. They get up at five in the morning, year in and year out. They struggle and strive all the days of their lives, merely to make ends meet, merely to keep the wolf from the door. Many of them do not even manage to do that, and these end their days in the poorhouse, notwithstanding that they have been gifted with fine libraries and beautiful parks and university endowments.

All the benevolence of all the philanthropists does not modify in the slightest degree the hard realities of production-for-profit industrialism. Capitalism continues remorselessly to grind the face of the poor, and will continue to do so while capitalism lasts.

Let us not deceive ourselves. The "elevation of the masses"—to use the cant phrase of the superior people—will not be brought about by philanthropy. Philanthropy may degrade; it cannot uplift. Carnegieism, in its later money-dispensing phase, can never undo the evil of its earlier money-getting phase. Carnegieism solves no problem, but it creates and intensifies problems innumerable, not the least of which has to do with the development of communal self-respect and dignity.

A community which is fated to carry through all its future history the taint of the Steel Trust bonds is hampered in that very element of spiritual and intellectual growth which it seems to be Mr. Carnegie's desire to foster. It inherits a tradition which must smell unwholesomely to the freer men of a better time. The people of the future will look with wonder and contempt upon all memorials of an economic slavery, the very existence of which it will be their aim to forget, and of whatever else in their history they may be proud, it will not be of their involuntary association with an economic monopoly, which typifies all the commercial craftiness of the nineteenth century with none of its chivalry.

Apart from these higher considerations, and looking to the mere utilitarian aspect of the question, history proves that all charitable endowments have a tendency to be diverted from their original purpose. Only the leisurely classes and the moneyed classes can partake to the full in either the recreative or the intellectual advantages conferred by Mr. Carnegie's benefactions. When the workers have better wages and shorter hours, and their lives are less completely absorbed by the mere struggle for existence, their thoughts will turn naturally to art and literature and nature, but by that time they will know how to get these things without dependence upon any rich man's well-intentioned whim.

As it is, every charitable gift helps to deepen their economic slavery, and it will be found that even in Mr. Carnegie's native town the enhancement of the value of the land surrounding the Pittencrieff estate will put money in the pockets of the speculators and increase the cost of living for the workers. Carnegieism, as I have said, solves nothing. It is rooted in economic injustice to begin with, and in the end, even when its motives are of the highest, it cannot help perpetuating the same kind of injustice.

The Man in the Street

Some little time ago—I think it was just about the time when those ridiculous swashbuckling Jameson Raiders gave us our first South African sensation—the man in the newspaper office, ever on the lookout for a catchy phrase, made a discovery. He discovered the "man in the street," and ever since that somewhat indefinable personage has been a valuable asset in modern journalism. He has strutted and posed and postured in the columns of the daily press, in sedate monthly magazines, and in the so-called comic papers on every possible occasion.

Never a public event has transpired but the imaginary opinion of this imaginary man in the street has been quoted as if it were an actual opinion easily ascertainable, and of some importance when ascertained. Politicians on both sides make appeal to him, and are at great pains to prove that the man in the street sports their particular party colours. He has been poetised, idealised, apostrophised, and caricatured, and, at least, one book has been dedicated to him. The man in the street has, in fact, well-nigh ousted our blustering friend, John Bull, from his time-honoured pre-eminence as the representative Britisher. The typical Englishman is no longer a burly, beef-eating, farmer man, with a "tight little island" for his home; but an under-sized city corner-boy, with a paper trumpet, a penny Union Jack, and a world-wide Empire. The change is symptomatic of much. I think there is some cause for misgiving in this phenomenal uplifting into prominence of the man in the street. I can understand some deference being paid to the man in the workshop, or the man behind the plough, or the man at the ballot-box, but the man in the street; who is he, or what is he? Is he anything else than a phrase, a mere penny-a-liner's figure of speech, signifying nothing, or is he a flesh and blood embodiment of any social principle? Is he a responsible, reasoning, and reasonable being? I think not; yet he may be all the more dangerous on that account.

I have noticed that in past times when the ruling classes had any particularly diabolical piece of mischief on hand they appealed to the man in the street. They did not call him by that name in those days. He was the populace, the people, the mob; the "voice of God" they even named him sometimes; and then set him to do the work of the devil. When the Roman Governor of a certain Jewish city wanted to divest himself of responsibility for the greatest judicial crime—at least the most far-reaching judicial crime on record—he turned to the man in the street. The man in the street did the dirty work and the Governor went out and washed his hands. Barabbas was chosen and Christ was crucified. He has been crucified many thousand times since—by the man in the street. So far as I have been able to observe, the man in the street to-day is the same man that he was then; an irresponsible; a puppet, dancing at the end of invisible wires manipulated from newspaper offices, political committee-rooms, and company directors' board-rooms; a puppet, but a dangerous one. He is a creature of whims, prejudices, passions; a reasonable being, never. The best that can be said of him is that he acts upon impulse. If by any chance a good impulse gains the mastery over him, then he is less harmful. He has been known to storm a Bastille and dethrone a tyrant, and also to perpetrate a Bartholomew massacre, but neither his good nor his evil deeds are the results of deliberate judgment. He worships the rising star, not the setting one. He follows the band. If there are two bands he follows the one with the biggest drum, the most resounding brass, and the strongest lung power. He shouts for Caesar one day and for Brutus the next.

He is no new phenomenon, the man in the street. He has been there ever since there was a street; since the first dawnings of what is called civilisation he has been there; and he is not civilised yet. He is the eternal barbarian.

He has not even developed beyond the primitive stage the instinct of self-preservation, and the very people who make of him a tool may shoot him in that street of which he is supposed to be the master, and he knows not how to defend himself. They may starve him and he will submit; ay, even though the shop-windows in his street are overflowing with food. He is the man in the street, that and nothing more. He lives there, and dies there in a narrow, contracted, jerry-built cubicle, specially designed for the man in the street. A barbarian, without the barbarian's sense of freedom or love of nature. The broad acres and fertile fields are not for him. They belong to his master. He is rigorously barred and wire-fenced out from the hills and valleys, and woodlands and streams. His place is the city pavement. Once in a while, on special days, ironically called holy-days, he is allowed to go out and look at the sun; to run about for a few hours on his master's hills, or paddle a canoe for a little on his master's lakes and rivers, but he has to get back to his street, and is usually glad to get back. It is the only place where he can feel at home. God pity the "man in the street," and God help the nation whose heart beats responsive to the waving of his trumpery Union Jack.

Vanity Fair

For my sins I have had put into my hands this week the Christmas number of a society paper. Its chief purpose is to chronicle the comings and goings, and sayings and posturings, of people who are "in society." I should say that it is a kind of window through which Lazarus, from afar off in his East End Hades, may gaze upon the doings of Dives in his West End Paradise; or shall we rather say that it is a multi-coloured kaleidoscopic reflection of Vanity Fair? It is certainly a strange, fantastic world which is here revealed; a world which the ordinary everyday man has grown so accustomed looking at from the outside—in much the same way that he looks upon the transformation scene in a pantomime—that he has ceased to realise its relationship to the world in which he himself lives. What has he to do with these gay butterflies of fashion, these social dancing dolls and court marionettes, these human monstrosities, to whom ceremonious frivolity is the serious business of life? What can it matter to him, for example, that at the Ladies' Banquet, where the Duke of Connaught presided, "Lady Kilmorey, in rich cream satin, embroidered in black, sat on the Duke's right hand," while "Lady Garvagh, in a dress of pale pink and lace, wore innumerable diamonds, including a big diamond bumble bee with flashing ruby eyes"? or that "the Duke and Duchess of Roxburghe will arrive in London on December 12, for some Christmas shopping"? or that the "King enjoyed his shooting at Rising Castle and walked well with the guns"?

These ongoings interest the average man only as a kind of show—a second-hand show—which he is permitted to view only through the fashion columns of his daily or weekly paper. And that is the pity of it, that he should be content to take the show for granted, just in the same way that he takes for granted the suffering and degradation of the poor, and the chronic discomfort of his own life.

Well, the show is here, or the shadow of it, here in the pages of the society paper, and I must confess that, sitting as I do in the heart of one of the most congested districts of a great city, this glimpse into that other world has for me a certain strange fascination. It is all so different, so bright, and joyous, and beautiful; so light and airy, and spacious, and seeming-comfortable compared with the stifling tenements, and dark closes, and dull streets and pinched unhappy children, that I feel positively grateful to the fashionmonger for making known to me that life is not altogether grey for everybody. It gives me pleasure to know that, despite the hard times, Christmas will be a merry Christmas for some folks; that "the Duke and Duchess of Sutherland with their children will spend the Christmas holidays at Dunrobin Castle," which I am told is a much more cheerful place than Whitechapel; that "Lord and Lady Algernon Gordon-Lennox will return home from America in time for Christmas"; and I feel quite sorry for the Earl and Countess of Yarmouth, who cannot "arrive back in England until the 29th," and will therefore be too late for the Christmas pudding, though doubtless the dancing Earl and his wife will have a gay enough time on board the Atlantic liner that brings them home.

Yes, it will be a merry Christmas—in society. An eating and drinking, dancing and junketing, frolicsome merry Christmas. And as at Christmas, so it is for these people all the year round. A perennial hunting after pleasure. A ceaseless career of inane, vapid uselessness. A never-ending wasteful dissipation of life's treasures and opportunities. It is all revealed here, in this society paper, this guide, philosopher, and friend to the frivolous populace of Vanity Fair. The bridge-playing, and polo-playing, and yachting, and racing, and hunting, the balls, and dinners, and Court ceremonies, and fashionable weddings, and all that empty shallow life which spends itself within the charmed circle of caste-erected barriers, by which these people have shut themselves in from the workaday world outside.

I suppose they are happy in a way, and as far as their ideal of happiness goes. The unfortunate young woman who last week began her married life in chains—chains of pearls—costing £60,000, must have been happy. She could not know the real cost of those pearls. She could not know their cost in human life and labour. She could not know that on her pretty shoulders were the year's earnings of one thousand men. She could not know that 60,000 little children in London were hungry because their father's labours had gone to produce pearls and other adornments instead of food. Truly the pearls of Vanity Fair are pearls of great price. Could she have known these things, I think she would not have been happy. I think so, because I believe that human nature is much the same in Vanity Fair as it is in Slumland. I am not at this season of goodwill preaching the doctrine of hatred. There are kindly souls in silks and satins, just as in rags and tatters, and the sin—if sin it be—of society, high and low, is not the sin of deliberate heartlessness, but of ignorance; ignorance which gives us thoughtlessness, pride and arrogance in Vanity Fair; slavishness, servility, and hopelessness in Slumland; and vulgarity in both.

Hatred? No! Why should we hate these foolish people? Like their forerunners of nineteen hundred years ago, "they know not what they do."

Yet we are bound to ask ourselves the question—Must this state of things continue for ever? Is there to be no ending to it? This is the same Vanity Fair pictured by

John Bunyan, satirised by Thackeray, preached at by Kingsley, thundered at by Carlyle, denounced by Ruskin, and which William Morris fought his life long to abolish. And here it is with us still, thriving and flourishing and flaunting its brazen barbarity in the face of honest folks; prostituting and commandeering to its service even the attributes of human progress, the triumphs of Art and Science, and of Religion itself, and polluting the social atmosphere of the whole nation.

And still on the other side of the wall lies that other city; the sad city of want and sorrow and suffering and grinding poverty. The riot of the one draws its sustenance from the toil and penury of the other. The sighs and moans of the one mingle with the songs and laughter of the other, and make mournful music enough in the ear of humanity.

And they are both built upon the same foundation, a foundation of economic injustice. Only when Socialism shall have done its work, when it shall have destroyed the foundation, only then will this age-long Tale of Two Cities come to an end, and the City of the Commonweal take the place of Vanity Fair.